VAN GOGH AT
THE VAN GOGH MUSEUM

Ossip Zadkine
Model for the statue of
Vincent and Theo van
Gogh

VAN GOGH AT
THE VAN GOGH MUSEUM

Ronald de Leeuw

Waanders Publishers | Zwolle

Contents

Introduction

The Van Gogh Museum

When, during a three-day excursion to Amsterdam in October 1885, Vincent van Gogh paid a visit to the recently opened Rijksmuseum, the young artist could not possibly have imagined that in less than a century, on 2 June 1973, an entire museum on Amsterdam's Museumplein would be dedicated to his own artistic legacy. In the two decades that have elapsed since its foundation, the Van Gogh Museum has grown into one of the most popular institutions of its kind in Europe, a place of pilgrimage for millions seeking the unique experience of standing face to face with one of the nineteenth century's most fascinating artists.

Though it was in France that Van Gogh lived and worked from 1886, and there that he carved out a place for himself in the annals of Post-impressionism, only a modest portion of his prodigious oeuvre remained in that country. After the artist's death, his brother Theo's widow took most of the unsold drawings and pictures back with her to Holland. Thanks in part to the superb collection that Hélène Kröller-Müller amassed in the early twentieth century, over a third of the master's oeuvre found a permanent home in his native land. Besides the museum that bears his name, the municipal museums of Amsterdam, The Hague and Rotterdam, as well as numerous smaller museums scattered about Holland, proudly preserve important Van Goghs.

The collection of the Van Gogh Museum in Amsterdam is far and away the largest and most representative of the artist's oeuvre. It includes seven sketchbooks and some six hundred original letters from Vincent to Theo, in addition to over two hundred paintings and 580 drawings, all on permanent loan from the Vincent van Gogh Foundation. The Museum also houses work by friends and colleagues which Theo, who dealt in art, and Vincent either purchased or acquired through exchange. This so-called Theo van Gogh Collection makes it possible to present the oeuvre of Vincent van Gogh in a broader context, while forming in turn the basis of the Museum's acquisition policy. Over the past few years the Van Gogh Museum has been actively redefining itself as an institution where, with Van Gogh as the pivotal figure, a broad swath of European art of the later nineteenth century is presented in all its diversity. In this respect the Museum forms an ideal link between its neighbours on the Museumplein: the Rijksmuseum, devoted primarily to Dutch fine and applied art up to approximately 1900, and the Stedelijk Museum, with its international twentieth-century collection.

At the time the Van Gogh Museum was founded, a museum dedicated to a single artist was still something of an anomaly. Since then the foundation of the Musée Picasso in Paris has

Meijer de Haan,
Portrait drawing of
Theo van Gogh
(1857-1891) in 1889

Official opening of the Van Gogh Museum by
H.M. Queen Juliana on 2 June 1973

dispelled any lingering doubts about the formula of the 'one-man museum' – provided, of course, that the appeal of the artist is sufficiently universal and that the quality of the collection does justice to his art. Indeed it is a rare, if not unique, luxury to be able to plumb the creative process of a great master so deeply in a single location – though one could hardly say the rest of the world is bereft of Van Gogh's work! Of the more than nine hundred pictures the artist is estimated to have painted in the course of his brief career, two thirds have found their way into public and private collections from Moscow to Melbourne, and from Toronto to Sao Paulo.

Amsterdam, however, is home to the core of Vincent's oeuvre. In the Van Gogh Museum there are entire ensembles from every period of the artist's creativity. The Brabant period is particularly well represented: almost all the major works, including the definitive version of *The Potato Eaters*, are still together, as is nearly everything Van Gogh is known to have painted during his brief Antwerp sojourn in 1885-86. Thanks to no less than eighty-five canvases, including an impressive series of eighteen self-portraits, the stylistic metamorphosis Van Gogh underwent in Paris can be studied here better than anywhere else. From Vincent's Arles period the Museum possesses such major works as *The Bedroom*, *The Yellow House*, the *Sunflowers* and what may well be his loveliest landscape, *Harvest at La Crau*. While this group is notably rich in landscapes, figure pieces and portraits are few and far between. There is unfortunately no *Arlésienne*, no *Berceuse*, no *Postman Roulin*. The artist's convalescence in St-Rémy is worthily represented by *The Reaper*, the *Vase with Irises* and the *Branches of an Almond Tree in Blossom*. Nor can so many of his unique copies after his favourite painter Millet be found

anywhere but Amsterdam. Four of the principal canvases from the last month of Van Gogh's life in Auvers form an impressive finale to the display: the atmospheric *View of the Castle of Auvers*, the revolutionary *Tree Roots*, the menacing *Landscape with Stormy Sky* and the *Cornfield with Crows* – formerly taken to be his swan song.

The caretakers of the estate

When Vincent van Gogh died in July 1890 he did not leave a will. In August 1890, however, his sisters Anna, Elisabeth and Willemien agreed that his brother Theo would inherit the entire estate. After all, Theo had supported Vincent for many years, thus enabling him to pursue an artistic career. When Theo died in turn on 25 January 1891, on behalf of his widow the sisters formally renounced any claim to the brothers' collection. Shortly thereafter Jo van Gogh-Bonger decided to leave Paris, and to take her infant son Vincent Willem to her native Holland. She settled in Bussum, where she took in lodgers and translated for a living. As the widow of an art dealer, she naturally supplemented her income by selling works from the collection from time to time. In 1901 Jo married the painter and critic Johan Cohen Gosschalk, who wholeheartedly supported her tireless struggle to promote her late brother-in-law's art. In 1903 the family moved to

Johan Cohen Gosschalk, Jo van Gogh-Bonger
(1862-1925) at her writing table

Jo Bonger, Johan Cohen Gosschalk and Vincent Willem van Gogh in the sittingroom of their house on Brachthuyzerstraat in Amsterdam, ca. 1905

Isaac Israëls, Vincent Willem van Gogh in Hyde Park, London, August 1914

Amsterdam. Cohen Gosschalk took an active part in organising the large Van Gogh exhibition at the Stedelijk Museum, which helped establish the artist's reputation. In 1910 the family returned to the country, where Cohen Gosschalk died in 1912. In 1914 Jo van Gogh-Bonger, who had reassumed her first husband's name in the meantime, put the finishing touches on what could well be called her life's work, an edition of the entire corpus of Vincent's letters to Theo. After completing his training as a civil engineer, in 1915 Jo and Theo's son, Vincent Willem, married Josina Wibaut. He was determined to demonstrate his own professional merits before becoming more actively involved with the Van Gogh Collection – which he had already begun to do while his mother was still alive. With few exceptions, nothing more was sold after Jo van Gogh died in 1925. In 1927 Dr Vincent Willem van Gogh and his wife settled in Laren, after their residence 't Lanthuys (The Country House), into which Jo had moved in 1910, had been radically remodelled. Twenty of Van Gogh's most famous pictures, most of them mounted in flat white frames, served as decoration; the rest were kept in a makeshift storage room. This situation changed in 1930, following another major exhibition at the Stedelijk Museum of works from the collections of Dr van Gogh and Hélène Kröller-Müller. When the exhibition closed, the former was asked to allow his Van Goghs to be displayed in the Stedelijk on a permanent basis. On 5 November 1930, thanks in part to the insistence of Josina van Gogh-Wibaut, the Van Gogh family and the Municipality reached a formal agreement to this effect. With the exception of the war years – when the collection was hidden in the dunes near the small town of Castricum – much of the collection was hung there on a semi-permanent basis. Dr van Gogh presented his uncle's *Berceuse* to the Stedelijk in gratitude for the Museum's care of the collection during the war.

In close consultation with the successive directors of the Stedelijk Museum, after World War II Vincent Willem began organising exhibitions of the collection in Europe, the United States and Canada during the winter months, which considerably enhanced Vincent's international renown. Eventually Dr van Gogh realised that if appropriate steps were not taken, the collection would be irretrievably dispersed after his death. In late 1959 H.J. Reinink, Director-General for the Arts at the Ministry of Education, Arts and Sciences, presented the engineer with a detailed proposal. The plan envisaged a museum especially for the collection in Amsterdam, which would be provided by the Dutch state. To this end the Vincent van Gogh Foundation was founded on 10

*Vincent van Gogh, La Berceuse, Stedelijk
Museum, Amsterdam*

July 1960. Besides Dr Vincent Willem van Gogh, his second
wife and his three children, a state representative also sits on
the board. With the consent of the Dutch parliament, the state
purchased the entire collection on behalf of the Foundation in
1962. The Municipality of Amsterdam furnished the land for
the museum on Museumplein.

*Sketch designs for the Van Gogh Museum by
Gerrit Rietveld, June 1963*

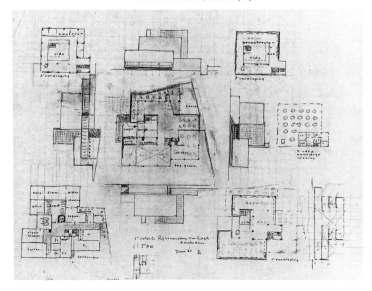

The Museum

In 1963 Dr van Gogh met for the first time with the architect of
his choice, Gerrit Rietveld, one of the foremost exponents of
the De Stijl movement, which had flourished in the 1920s.
Frank Lloyd Wright's recently completed Guggenheim
Museum in New York formed an important source of
inspiration, as did the Maison de la Culture in Le Havre by
Le Corbusier's pupil Audigier, noted for its flexible
arrangement of space and natural lighting. In 1964 Rietveld
died, however, as did his successor, J. van Dillen, in 1966. At
that point their associate J. van Tricht was contracted for the
definitive design of the building and its interior. The original
plan was to cover the Museum with off-white glazed (or
clinker) bricks and brownish grey enamelled steel sheets. For
various, primarily practical reasons this plan was abandoned,
however, in favour of grey blocks composed of concrete chips;
this accounts for the massive, impregnable appearance of the
building from the street.

Given the somewhat forbidding exterior, visitors are all the
more surprised by the interior of the Museum, with its series
of airy, interconnected spaces flooded with daylight from an
immense central well covered with glass. The well creates an
extraordinary spatial effect that is conducive to an
uninhibited, relaxed encounter with the works of art. This
same central column of air enables the building, originally
designed for sixty to eighty thousand visitors per year, to
accommodate over ten times that number with none of the
claustrophobia one would expect.
The founders' original intention had been to display the
relatively dark works from Vincent's Brabant period on the
ground floor, and the sunnier canvases from the French
period on the higher floors, nearer the skylight, but for
various reasons this proved impractical. As things now stand
a rotating selection of nineteenth-century pictures is usually
displayed on the ground floor of the Museum, while the
monumental first floor is entirely given over to a
chronological presentation of the artist's principal works.
This enables the visitor to follow Van Gogh's development
through the various stages of his life, as he moved from
Nuenen to Antwerp, then on to Paris, Arles, St-Rémy and
finally to Auvers-sur-Oise.

Originally the second floor, which is protected from daylight,
was set aside for a permanent selection of Vincent's drawings
and for the collection of Japanese prints he and Theo

Exterior of the Van Gogh Museum seen from Museumplein

assembled. But since the increasingly stringent international standards of collection management militate against exposing works on paper to light, however weak, for extended periods of time, Van Gogh's drawings are now displayed only in temporary exhibitions. Even stricter rules apply to his extremely fragile letters. Written for the most part in corrosive iron gall ink on inexpensive paper, these brittle sheets are exceedingly fragile. Only for the centenary of the artist's death in 1990 was an exception made, when all the illustrated letters were featured in a moving exhibition. Part of the space on the second floor is now reserved for a study collection: a wide selection of Van Gogh's minor works which are usually kept in storage, presented informally. In 1990, during the large-scale retrospective exhibition commemorating the 100th anniversary of Vincent's death, no less than 865,000 visitors visited the Museum. Not only the air conditioning but also the lighting of the building had to be specially adapted for the occasion. As we noted in the case of graphic art, the amount of light to which oil paintings may be exposed has also been greatly reduced since the building's construction in 1973. Under the guidance of the architect Frank Wintermans, a number of aesthetic adjustments were made to the interior on that occasion. A layer of stucco was applied to the walls of the central, glass-covered well to give it a more streamlined appearance, for instance.

The two most dominant structural elements of the building – the stairways in the glass-covered centre of the building and on the side facing Museumplein – serve to channel the flow of visitors. That in the centre enables one to experience the interior as a whole, while that on the side commands a fine view of Museumplein. Each floor can also be reached by lift, so that the building is fully accessible to the handicapped. As it was designed by Rietveld, Van Dillen and Van Tricht, the Museum has coped remarkably well under the circumstances. Every building has its limits, however. The steadily rising tide of visitors has left no choice but to add a wing. Their numbers

Letter from Vincent van Gogh to Theo, Arles, May 1888

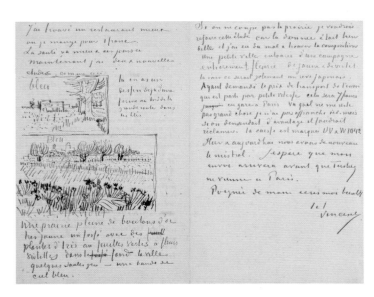

The study collection on the second floor of the Van Gogh Museum

have grown by an average of fifty thousand every year since 1985, mostly concentrated during the summer months. In order to guarantee every interested individual an equally rewarding, relaxed visit, more square feet are required. From the mid-1980s the rapid succession of temporary exhibitions exacerbated the need for space designated especially for this purpose.

In late 1989 the Amsterdam City Council granted the Van Gogh Museum permission to expand on the side facing Museumplein. In the autumn of 1991, the financial basis for the expansion was laid when 37.5 million Dutch guilders were donated by the Yasuda Fire & Marine Insurance Company Ltd., the same Japanese insurance firm that had caused an international sensation several years earlier when it purchased one of the three versions of Van Gogh's *Still Life with Sunflowers* for a record sum. The company's donation to the Museum underscores its association with the artist, who is immensely popular in Japan. The Japanese architect Kisho Kurokawa was asked to design the new exhibition wing.

Kisho Kurokawa, Design for the expansion of the Van Gogh Museum (1991)

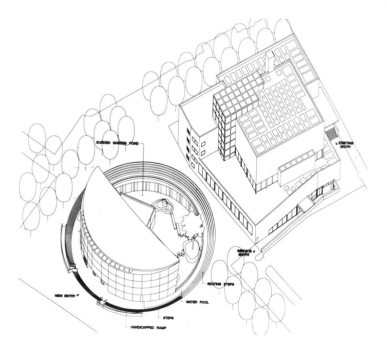

The evolution of the collection since 1973

Acquisitions are the lifeblood of every museum. A collection is a living organism fed constantly by new impulses, a repository of art and knowledge that constantly grows and improves. Be it a museum with a historically defined parameter such as our own or a museum of contemporary art, this process continues indefinitely. Since most Dutch museums have done very little collecting in the field of international nineteenth-century painting in recent decades, the Van Gogh Museum decided to accept the challenge. In formulating an acquisition policy, the Museum has taken the character of the core collection as its point of departure, acquiring works consistent with or complementary to the collection the Van Gogh brothers assembled. The brothers' correspondence tells us a great deal about their taste, thus forming an invaluable guideline. In a more general sense, the Museum also seeks to enrich the artistic patrimony of the Netherlands in the field of European painting from the period 1840-1920. The related collection of the H.W. Mesdag Museum in The Hague, administered by the Van Gogh Museum since 1990, influences the acquisition policy as well. Vincent and Theo van Gogh lacked both the time and the means that would have enabled their instincts as collectors to mature. In the span of a few short years they amassed what

Georges Seurat, A l'Eden-Concert - 1887

Vincent van Gogh, The Zouave (1888)

could be described as a typical artist's collection, consisting largely of works acquired through exchange with colleagues such as Bernard, Gauguin, Guillaumin, Pissarro and Toulouse-Lautrec. Only a small portion of their collection – the groups of works by Monticelli and Gauguin, the Manet prints and the splendid Seurat drawing – was actually purchased.

With the opening of the Van Gogh Museum in 1973, it finally became possible to study and enjoy the collection in its entirety, with all its strengths and weaknesses. Thanks to Dr van Gogh's foresight, this was one private collection that made the transition to a museum without being allowed to fossilise. From the outset he took the position that the collection was a living organism that needed to grow. Between 1962 and his death in 1978 he was actively involved in purchasing works by Van Gogh and his contemporaries, to the extent that he occasionally advanced his own funds when government approval took too long. Besides the half dozen drawings and several small paintings by Van Gogh that he acquired for the Museum, he successfully sollicited a number

Léon Lhermitte,
The Haymakers (La fenaison), 1887

of gifts and legacies. As a result, the Van Gogh Museum could present its namesake as an artist engaged in a lively dialogue with the art of his age, as opposed to 'le grand isolé'.

In the years that immediately followed the Museum's opening, Van Gogh's work did not fetch the sort of astronomical sums regularly reported in the press nowadays, and an occasional acquisition was still within the realm of possibility. In 1977 the Museum purchased Vincent's *Poplars in the Autumn* from his Nuenen period and in 1979 the powerful portrait drawing *The Zouave*. Since such acquisitions were long since out of

the question by 1990, that year's bequest of two small pictures from the estate of Mrs E. Ribbius Peletier, which Dr van Gogh had arranged before he died, was particularly gratifying. Most works that enter the Museum nowadays are acquired with funds generated by the museum shop. In addition purchases are made with the support of the Vincent van Gogh Foundation. On several occasions an appeal has been made to the Vereniging Rembrandt or to the Ministry of Welfare, Public Health and Culture. The Museum has also received gifts and

*Claude Monet,
Bulb Fields and
Windmills near
Rijnsburg, 1886*

Thomas Couture, A Realist (Un Réaliste), 1865

bequests from private individuals, the business community
and the Friends of the Van Gogh Museum Foundation.

Two acquisition areas that have received particular attention
are Realism and Symbolism. While the Museum still has to do
without a picture by Millet, it boasts important pieces by his
colleagues Jules Breton, Jozef Israëls and Léon Lhermitte,
who likewise specialised in the peasant genre. The scant
representation of true Impressionist masters remains a thorn
in the Museum's side. When, therefore, in 1991 the Rijksdienst
Beeldende Kunst lent Claude Monet's *Bulb Fields* of 1886,
our joy was that much more intense.

Documentation and scientific research

As well as the numerous sketchbooks, drawings and paintings
of Vincent van Gogh, the Van Gogh Museum houses virtually
all of the letters the artist ever sent his brother Theo. It
preserves his scrapbooks, several of the albums he filled with
poetry for his brother, and the hundreds of magazine
illustrations he accumulated as a source of inspiration
throughout his life. The Vincent van Gogh Foundation has
lent the Museum a great deal of correspondence and archival
material relating to Theo van Gogh and other members of his
family. The archive of the Belgian Van Gogh connoisseur

Letter of Paul Gauguin to Vincent van Gogh from ca. 8 November 1889

Mark Edo Tralbaut has been moved to the Museum, moreover. Last but not least, there is an extensive library, which is especially strong in late nineteenth-century art; the library was immeasurably enriched in 1992, when the library of the Amsterdam artist's association Arti et Amicitiae was added to it. These various holdings make the Van Gogh Museum the preeminent place to study the artist and the reception of his oeuvre.

Starting in 1970 – that is, three years before the opening of the Museum – results of research carried out by the staff were routinely published in the *Bulletin Vincent*, for which the Van Gogh connoisseur Dr Jan Hulsker was largely responsible. By the time the *Bulletin* was discontinued in 1976, a total of sixteen issues had seen the light. In 1988, in collaboration with the Vincent van Gogh Foundation, the Museum launched a scholarly series entitled *Cahiers Vincent*, featuring previously unpublished sources that contribute in some way to our understanding of the artist. Individual *Cahiers* have included everything from poetry albums assembled by Vincent in the 1870s for his brother and various friends, to letters of condolence Theo received following his brother's death and research into the early provenance of Van Gogh's work. A study of Vincent's painting technique and materials has also appeared in the series.

Every year the Van Gogh Museum receives literally hundreds of requests for authentications of works of art from people hoping to hear they own a genuine Van Gogh, the vast majority of which are disappointed. The fact is that most of the submissions are all too patently unworthy of the artist, and indeed some prove to have been intentionally falsified. By the end of the last century Van Gogh's reputation was already such that it was worth forging his work.

Jo van Gogh and her son published what would remain the standard edition of Van Gogh's letters until 1973. That year Dr van Gogh ushered the last reprinting through the press, in time for the opening of the Van Gogh Museum. He himself was interested in editing the group of forty-five letters Gauguin wrote Vincent, Theo and Jo van Gogh, now preserved in the Museum, but could not finish the task before he died in 1978. Douglas Cooper finally published the correspondence in 1983, in co-operation with the Museum. In 1990 the staff of the Museum published a completely revised, Dutch-language edition of all known letters to and from Vincent van Gogh, based on new transcriptions. Since then they have been preparing a fully annotated edition of the entire correspondence, and there are also plans for a new catalogue raisonné of Van Gogh's oeuvre.

Exhibitions

After the opening of the Van Gogh Museum, the first director, Emile Meijer, was quick to introduce the fledgling institution to Amsterdam. Rather than limiting himself to Van Gogh and nineteenth-century art, he launched a wide range of activities, including concerts and theatrical productions. Mikis Theodorakis presented an anthology of his poetry in the Museum, and World Press Photo organised several of its annual exhibitions there as well. In the framework of a visual arts workshop the first courses were offered to the public on drawing, painting and photography.

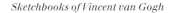

Sketchbooks of Vincent van Gogh

During Johannes van der Wolk's tenure as director (1978-1982), the Museum charted a more strictly art historical course. In conformity with the intentions of the founders, two important exhibitions – *Vincent van Gogh in his Dutch Years* (1980) and *Van Gogh and the Birth of Cloisonnism* (1981) – shed valuable light on the artistic context in which Van Gogh worked. The Van Gogh retrospective exhibition in 1990, which was organised in co-operation with the Rijksmuseum Kröller-Müller, was of course a milestone in this respect. The artist was also featured in such exhibitions as *Van Gogh & Millet* (1989) and *Van Gogh and Modern Art 1890-1914* (1990), but by the time Ronald de Leeuw became director in 1986, the Museum's focus had expanded to include the entire second half of the nineteenth century, which it approached, moreover, not from a Dutch or French, but from an international perspective. The Van Gogh Museum also collaborated on numerous exhibitions abroad, including pioneering Van Gogh exhibitions in Toronto, New York, Paris and Arles. The Museum itself organised exhibitions in Italy and Japan, often in co-operation with the Rijksmuseum Kröller-Müller.

Most exhibitions in the Van Gogh Museum naturally revolve around French artists, who set the tone in nineteenth-century Europe, after all, as well as the standard by which Van Gogh judged art: 'don't they form the heart of this century as far as painting is concerned?' he asked.

Since the mid-1980s, the Museum has also frequently focused on facets of late nineteenth-century graphic art, which went through so many turbulent innovations.
Apart from loan exhibitions selections from the Museum's own collection of works on paper are regularly presented, such as Manet prints or English wood engravings originally acquired by the Van Gogh brothers. Japanese graphic art and Japonisme are commonly featured; after all, Van Gogh was one of the principal exponents of the island nation's art, which captivated the contemporary European art world. In 1978 Dr W. van Gulik prepared an initial catalogue of the Museum's own collection of Japanese woodcuts. Then in 1991 a new edition of the catalogue, which was entirely revised and supplemented, was published by Charlotte van Rappard.

When the Van Gogh Museum was established, Dr van Gogh stipulated that it operate according to the most advanced standards, but he was equally concerned that it be a lively institution. Visitors should be confronted not only with the work of Van Gogh, he thought, but also with that of other

Edouard Manet, Les courses (The Races), litho 1865/72

nineteenth-century artists, in either the permanent collection or in temporary exhibitions. It is with this brief in mind that the present volume intentionally surrounds the work of Vincent van Gogh with that of his colleagues Emile Bernard and Paul Gauguin. The book thus seeks to acquaint the reader with the 'entourage d'amis et d'artistes' whose work the Van Gogh brothers personally admired, notwithstanding the second thoughts they had about some of them. The brothers' collection and indeed their legacy continues to evolve under the constant care of the Museum's staff. They draw inspiration from one of Vincent's own remarks in a letter he wrote Theo in January 1874: *'admire as many works of art* as you can, most people *don't admire enough'*.

Preface

Although the Van Gogh Museum also preserves more than a thousand drawings, sketchbook sheets, letter illustrations and prints by Vincent van Gogh and the artists of his century, the illustrations selected for this volume were limited to works in oil, pastel or watercolour.

All of the works illustrated form part of the permanent collection of the Van Gogh Museum, unless otherwise indicated, and are arranged in accordance with Van Gogh's biography corresponding to the various stages of his artistic pilgrimage: the successive sojourns in The Hague, Drenthe, Nuenen, Antwerp, Paris, Arles, St-Rémy and Auvers-sur-Oise. The book also focuses on two of Van Gogh's closest colleagues, Emile Bernard and Paul Gauguin.

Van Gogh's works are often described through quotations from the artist's correspondence. The translated excerpts from the letters are based on the integral Dutch-language edition published by the Van Gogh Museum, De brieven van Vincent van Gogh (1990). So as not to encumber the text unnecessarily, the precise origins of these quotations is not indicated. However, the dates of the letters quoted, mostly to his brother Theo, are stated whenever possible, so that they can be traced without difficulty.

The inventory number of every work has been provided.

The significance of the various letters is as follows:

S: painting
D: drawing, watercolour or pastel
P: print
V: object or sculpture

M: property of the Van Gogh Museum
V: property of the Vincent van Gogh Foundation, on permanent loan to the Van Gogh Museum
F: the number assigned to the work in J.-B. de la Faille, The Works of Vincent van Gogh. His Paintings and Drawings, Amsterdam 1970

The year at the end of each inventory number indicates when the work entered the Museum, be it as a gift, a loan or a purchase.

Van Gogh in The Hague and Drenthe

In late December 1881 Van Gogh moved into a small flat just off The Hague's Schenkweg, 'about ten minutes behind Mauve'. He expected a great deal from the lessons he was to get from his cousin Anton Mauve and from his contact with the younger members of the Hague School. However things did not go according to plan. Mauve was very helpful at first, but the two artists tended to get on each other's nerves. Nor did Vincent's liaison with the pregnant prostitute Sien Hoornik do anything to improve his choleric cousin's opinion of him. H.G. Tersteeg, the influential art dealer who managed Goupil's branch in The Hague, turned against the novice as well. In the end the cousins parted ways. It was while he was still under Mauve's tutelage that Vincent painted his first picture, *Still Life with Cabbage and Clogs*. Yet most of his time in The Hague was spent drawing. His uncle, the art dealer C.M. van Gogh, gave the aspirant his first commission: twelve views of The Hague in pen and ink. A series of lithographs inspired by the 'Heads of the People', he had seen in the English magazine *The Graphic*, was undertaken but never finished.

When his relationship with Sien finally deteriorated and his finances showed no sign of improvement, Vincent decided to move to the Dutch province of Drenthe in the northeastern part of the country. He later avowed that he had taken this rather 'hasty' decision in the hope of finding 'something of the strict poetry of the real moors'. His colleague Anthon van Rappard had worked in the region previously, and on 13 August 1882, long before his departure for the province, Van Gogh wrote him about it: 'What you said about Drenthe interests me. I know absolutely nothing about it personally, but only what Mauve and Termeulen, among others, brought with them. I imagine it being like North Brabant *when I was young*, about 20 years ago [...]'. Having concentrated on urban themes while living in The Hague, Van Gogh reverted to landscapes and country life in Drenthe. Judging from the twenty-two letters he sent Theo from the province, he was terribly lonely. It had apparently pained him to leave Sien behind in The Hague. 'Theo, when I see such a poor woman on the heath with a child on her arm or at her breast, my eyes get moist. I'm reminded of her; her weakness and untidiness only make the likeness greater'. By early December the solitude had become too much for him: '*that* loneliness, encountered by a painter who in the middle of nowhere is taken by every Tom, Dick and Harry for a madman, murderer, vagabond, etc. etc.' He decided to return to Brabant, to live with his parents in Nuenen.

During the month of September 1882 Van Gogh occasionally attempted to produce a 'saleable' watercolour. The letter sketch with four locals sitting on a bench under a tree in The Hague is an example of these. Several weeks later he wrote Theo about it: 'Recently I've been painting almost nothing but watercolours. [...] Perhaps you remember Moorman's State Lottery Office at the top of Spuistraat? I passed by one rainy morning when a crowd of people were waiting to buy tickets. [...] I was struck by their expressions of anticipation and as I was working, they took on a greater, deeper significance than they had had at first. [The subject] becomes more meaningful, I think, if one interprets it as *the poor and money*'.

Vincent van Gogh
Beach at Scheveningen
Canvas, 34.5 × 51 cm - 1882
Inv. S 416 M/1990 - F 4

Marine and beach views have always been popular motifs in Dutch painting. Following the great florescence of the genre in the seventeenth century, the sea's beauty was rediscovered in the early nineteenth. In their turn, painters of the Hague School such as Jacob Maris, Hendrik Willem Mesdag and J.H. Weissenbruch upheld this tradition. The picturesque fishing village of Scheveningen was only a stone's throw from The Hague, and some artists chose to live within easy reach of the beach. Indeed Van Gogh's flat just off the Schenkweg was within minutes of it. His colleague Bernard Blommers let him store his materials in his studio in Scheveningen. This beach view is one of the first paintings Van Gogh ever made, and he was pleasantly surprised by the results. 'I thought the first things would look like nothing', he confessed.

No more than the members of the Hague School did he object to working outdoors in bad weather. The beach view was captured shortly before 'an angry storm', when the sea was the colour of 'dirty dishwater'.

Vincent van Gogh
Landscape in Drenthe with Canal and Sailboat
Pencil, pen, ink, heightened with white,
31.2 × 42.3 cm - autumn 1883
Inv. D 810 M/1986 - F 1104
Acquired with the support of the Vereniging
Rembrandt

'I see no way to describe the [Drenthe] landscape as it ought to be described, since words fail me. But imagine the banks of the canal as miles and miles of Michels or Th. Rousseaus, for instance, Van Goyens or Ph. de Konincks. Flat planes or strips, of different colours, which become narrower and narrower as they approach the horizon, accentuated here and there by a turf hut or small farm or a couple of gaunt birches, poplars, oaks – everywhere piles of turf and barges sailing by with peat or flag from the marshes'. The modern world had not yet encroached upon the moors of isolated Drenthe. Though factories and trains do figure in Van Gogh's landscapes later in his career, in Drenthe he delighted in an environment 'where things haven't got any further than stagecoaches and canalboats, where *everything is much less spoiled than any place I've ever seen*'. Time and again he was surprised by 'all the variety in the seemingly monotonous countryside'. In the late

Vincent van Gogh
Heath at Nightfall
Watercolour, 41.5 × 53.7 cm - September 1883
Inv. D 386 M/1977 - F 1099

afternoon especially the light changed and the landscape became 'sublime', which explains why Vincent captured most of his views of Drenthe just prior to sunset. He worked not only in oil and watercolour but also in ink, 'with a view to the painting, because one can go into much greater detail with the pen than with the brush'.

Though this lovely Drenthe watercolour recalls work by members of the Hague School who excelled at the technique, Van Gogh drew most of his inspiration from French art during the months he spent in Drenthe: 'Think of Barbizon, that's a marvellous story. Those who started out there – not all of them were by any means what they seemed to be. The countryside formed them. All they knew is: "it's no good in the city, I've got to get out [...]. I'm going to renew myself in the country"'.

Vincent van Gogh
Farmhouses
Canvas, 35 × 55.5 cm - September 1883
Inv. S 53 V/1962 - F 17

Though desolate Drenthe was not particularly popular among artists, several of Van Gogh's confrères had preceded him to the outstretched moors of this northeastern Dutch province. His awareness of this precedent is evinced by his account of an excursion to picturesque Zweeloo, 'the village where [the German painter] Liebermann stayed for a long time and made studies for his picture of the last [Paris] Salon, with the washing women. Where Termeulen and Jules Bakhuyzen spent a lot of time'. Van Gogh's cousin Anton Mauve and his friend Anthon van Rappard had worked in Drenthe as well. Yet the painters he most often mentioned were those of the Barbizon School, especially Daubigny, Dupré and Michel. It was with their work in mind

that he explored the Drenthe countryside. Of the work Vincent produced during his three months in the province, between 11 September and 5 December 1883, little actually survives. We know of only five canvases, three of which are preserved by the Van Gogh Museum.

Farmhouses may be one of the first paintings Vincent sent Theo, in late September. The houses themselves, which barely protrude above the boggy moors, are characteristically constructed out of turf, moss and reed, and actually embedded in the ground. The artist's memory of a work by Dupré in the collection of the Hague painter H.W. Mesdag doubtless influenced the final result: '[a canvas] showing two cottages, their mossy roofs of a surprisingly deep

tone against a hazy, dusty evening sky'. The other illustrated canvas with a house of this kind – 'with a delicate green cornfield in the foreground, withered grasses behind the house and piles of peat' – was painted several weeks later.

Whereas his friend Van Rappard had painted a characteristic old woman from Drenthe, Van Gogh had difficulty finding models willing to sit for him. Indeed the illustrated oil sketch of two women digging peat constitutes the only figure piece he is known to have painted in the province. The women, who are little more than silhouettes, are reminiscent of Millet's *Gleaners*, while the evening sky recalls the French master's equally famous *Angelus*.

Vincent van Gogh
Farmhouse with Peat-stacks
Canvas, 37.5 × 55.5 cm - October/November 1883
Inv. S 130 V/1962 - F 22

Vincent van Gogh
Two Women in a Peat-field
Canvas, 27.5 × 36.5 cm - October 1883
Inv. S 129 V/1962 - F 19

On 31 December 1883 a certain notary in Nuenen by the name of Schutjes organised a lumber sale, and Van Gogh recorded the event.

The sign of the inn where the auction was held can be seen on the left. The notary is clearly visible on a small platform at the back of the crowd. In early 1884 Vincent wrote Theo about a drawing he had made, 'though only an impression, of a lumber sale'. The motif calls to mind the scene of people gathered in front of the State Lottery Office in The Hague, which Van Gogh drew in 1882. Rather than painting this watercolour on the spot, the artist probably did so in the studio, with the help of sketches.

Van Gogh was presumably familiar with a watercolour of a similar subject – a lumber sale in a forest – by his cousin Anton Mauve, now in the Museum Hendrik Willem Mesdag in The Hague.

Van Gogh in Nuenen and Antwerp

Ringed by outstretched moors, Nuenen lies several kilometres southeast of Eindhoven, in the heart of Brabant. In late 1883, a total of 2,560 people lived in the village. Half of the labour force were farm workers, the other half cottage weavers.

Though South Brabant was (and is) predominantly Roman Catholic, there was a small Protestant congregation in Nuenen. In March 1875 Reverend Theodorus van Gogh, the father of Vincent, was offered the rectorate of Nuenen. There was also a vacancy in the village of Etten-Leur, however, which he chose instead. But when, in late 1881, the Nuenen rectorate became available once again, Reverend van Gogh finally relented, and formally assumed his responsibilities on 12 August 1882.

On about 5 December 1883 Vincent van Gogh arrived in Nuenen. Since his relationship with his parents had been deteriorating, his arrival was not a particularly happy occasion. Vincent knew they dreaded having a maladjusted artist – like 'a big shaggy dog' – around the house.

'He'll come into the room with wet paws, and he's so shaggy. He'll get in everyone's way. *And he barks so loud.* In short, he's a filthy beast'. The first fourteen days were rather awkward, but a frank conversation cleared the air somewhat and on 20 December 1883 Reverend van Gogh wrote his son Theo that it had 'gradually got better, especially since we agreed to his staying with us so he could make some studies here. He hoped the mangle room could be furnished for him; we don't think that's really a suitable place to live, but we've had a decent heater put into it [...]. So we're facing this new test in good spirits essentially, and have decided not to do anything about his peculiar clothes and so forth. By now the people here have seen him and though it's still a pity that he doesn't act more obliging, there's no changing his eccentricity. He certainly works hard and finds more than enough material here for studies, several of which we find quite beautiful'.

Vincent van Gogh
The Garden of the Vicarage in Nuenen in Winter: 'Mélancholie'
Pencil and ink, 29 × 21 cm - December 1883
Inv. D 87 V/1962

Vincent van Gogh
Weaver in his Loom
Pencil and watercolour, 32 × 44 cm - 1884
Inv. D 85 V/1962 - F 1125

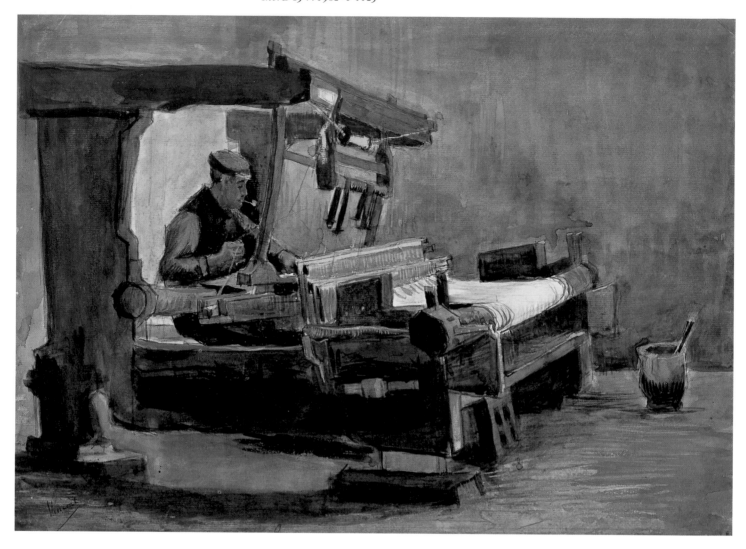

While living in The Hague, Van Gogh had read in Michelet's *Le Peuple* (1846) that the textile industry was responsible for creating 'a pathetic, misshapen kind of machine people, who were only capable of leading half a life'.
The artist himself described the weavers he witnessed in Nuenen as 'very pathetic little people', an impression the statistics confirm. As a rule the weavers lived at subsistence level and were decidedly poorer than the peasant population, who themselves could hardly be described as well off. In a letter written in September 1880 from the Borinage, Van Gogh already expressed compassion for the weavers, 'compared to other workers and artisans, a totally different sort of people'. He was moved by their 'dreamy, absent faces, like sleepwalkers'. They were 'the lowest of the low, so to speak, and the most despised'. In George Eliot's *Silas Marner* (1861), which Van Gogh read in 1876 and 1878, the weavers are described as pale runts who, compared to the robust country folk, looked like the last surviving members of an underprivileged race.

Between December 1883 and June 1884 Van Gogh busily depicted the weaving, yarn-spinning and reeling Brabanters, who comprised a quarter of Nuenen's labour force. In January 1884 he wrote: 'These people are difficult to draw, the rooms being so small that it's impossible to get far enough away to sketch the loom'. Nonetheless he managed to record the machinery with surprising technical precision. 'I'm also painting a loom – made of old, greenish, browned oak – on which the year *1730* is carved. Near that loom, at a small window looking out on a green plot, is a baby's chair. The child sits in it for hours, watching the shuttle fly to a fro'. In the evening they went on working by the light of an oil lamp, thus creating 'very Rembrandtesque effects'. Van Gogh tenderly recalled the old-fashioned 'lamp, like the one in Millet's *La Veillée*, for instance', which a weaver had once given him.

Vincent van Gogh
Weaver in his Loom
Pencil and watercolour, 35 × 45 cm - 1884
Inv. D 371 V/1962 - F 1114

Vincent van Gogh
Man Winding Yarn
Watercolour, 46.7 × 34 cm - 1884
Inv. D 387 V/1977 - F 1140

Vincent van Gogh
Spinning Wheel
Oil on canvas, 34 × 44 cm - 1884
Inv. S 54 V/1963 - F 175

Van Gogh's father was the sole
Protestant parson in a predominantly
Roman Catholic community. Only four
percent of the inhabitants of Nuenen
was Protestant. The small church
where the Reverend Van Gogh
officiated, built in 1824, is still standing.
Vincent made a painting of it for his
mother in January 1884. Initially he
placed a peasant with a spade over his
shoulder in the foreground, only to
overpaint the figure later with a group
of believers leaving the church after a
service.

Van Gogh executed the small picture of
the parsonage not long before he left
Nuenen, in October 1885. He had lived
there himself between December 1883
and the following May, during which
period he made several beautiful drawings of the garden.

The artist never mentioned the canvas
with the parsonage in his letters, unlike
the large illustrated landscape which he
described as 'a rather large study of a
road lined with poplars with yellow
autumn leaves, the sun casting bright
spots on the fallen leaves on the ground,
which alternate with the long shadows
of the trunks. At the end of the road [is
seen] a small peasant house with blue
sky above it, amid the autumn leaves'.
In the same letter of late October 1884,
Vincent reflected on 'impressionism',
which Theo had written him about. In
Paris, he realised, 'pictures are
beginning to be painted in a very
different tone than they were some
years ago'. His own palette still differed
radically from the chromatic ideal of the
innovators in France. Indeed he
predicted his own work would 'get a bit
gloomier sooner than it would get
lighter'.

Vincent van Gogh
Leaving the Church
at Nuenen
*Canvas, 41.5 × 32 cm -
1884*
Inv. S 03 V/1962 - F 25

Vincent van Gogh
Avenue of Poplars in
Autumn
*Canvas on panel,
98.5 × 66 cm - 1884
Inv. S 141 M/1977 -
F 122*

In Nuenen, between painting landscapes and scenes from peasant life, Van Gogh created over a dozen still lifes. The genre was apparently compatible with teaching a number of amateur painters, which he did in Eindhoven in exchange for tubes of paint. As he wrote his brother in November 1884, 'I now have three people in Eindhoven who want to learn to paint. I'm teaching them how to make still lifes'. His pupils included a goldsmith turned antique dealer by the name of Hermans (for whose house he had designed a decoration), the tanner Anton Kerssemakers and the postal worker Willem van de Wakker. Some of Van de Wakker's recollections of Vincent's instruction survive. It seems they met through a paint dealer by the name of Baaiens, whom the artist patronised. While studying under Anton Mauve, Van Gogh's own first picture had been a still life. According to Van de Wakker, he impressed upon his pupils that 'Painting still lifes is the start of everything. If you can do a still life, you can also do a forest'.

Van Gogh's ideal of a still-life painter was the eighteenth-century Frenchman Jean-Siméon Chardin, whose predilection for humble, everyday objects he shared. Though Van de Wakker recalled that in Eindhoven, Van Gogh borrowed antiques from his pupil Hermans's collection for his still lifes, it was the simplest that he invariably chose: bottles, boxes, pots and stoneware tankards. Painting these modest objects was all Van Gogh needed to test the French colour theories he had been reading about. Indeed when discussing colour theory with his Dutch colleagues, he indicated the colours in French.

Vincent van Gogh
Still Life with Pottery, Bottles and a Box
Canvas, 31 × 41 cm - 1884
Inv. S 60 V/1962 - F 61 recto

Vincent van Gogh
Still Life with Three Beer Mugs
Canvas, 32 × 43 cm - 1885
Inv. S 96 V/1962 - F 49

Vincent van Gogh
Still Life with Pottery and Three Bottles
Canvas, 39 × 56 cm - 1885
Inv. S 138 V/1962 - F 53

Vincent van Gogh
Still Life with Honesty (sketch belonging to
letter 493 of 5 April 1885)

Vincent van Gogh
Vase with Honesty
Canvas, 42.5 × 31.5 cm - 1884
Inv. S 09 V/1962 - F 76

The still life with the 'honesty and withered leaves against blue', which Van Gogh mentions in a letter of about 1 April 1885, can probably be identified with the illustrated canvas. The artist's uncle, the dealer C.M. van Gogh, had criticised the work, prompting him to make another attempt. A mere four days later he sketched the second version in a letter to Theo dated 5 April. The contents of the letter suggest that his brother had taken the first version of the still life with him when he left Nuenen at the end of a previous visit. Vincent's sketch of the still life in his letter to Theo is one of the few of its kind that he made in watercolour. In effect it is an homage to his father, who had died unexpectedly on March 26th: 'the objects in the foreground are a tobacco pouch and a pipe that belonged to Pa'. The painting no longer exists as it was later painted over by the artist. In September 1885 he used the canvas to paint a still life with apples. The only remaining eulogy to Rev. van Gogh is the still life *Open Bible, Extinguished Candle and Novel*, painted in the autumn of 1885.

In the winter of 1884/85 Van Gogh painted no less than forty studies of Nuenen peasant heads. After the series published in the English magazine *The Graphic* he entitled them 'Heads of the People'. In October 1884 he had written his brother of wanting to paint about thirty, and by November he had already painted some fifty of them. The entire series he hoped to finish by January 1885. Vincent approached these studies as training for a career as a portraitist: 'There is more and more demand for portraits – and there are not so many who can do them. I want to try and learn how to paint a head with character'. Creating an exact likeness was not his primary goal; rather, he strove to capture whatever was characteristic, which is what he admired about the heads of Daumier.

His taste ran to models with something Millet-like about them: 'crude, flat faces with low foreheads and thick lips – not that sharpness, but full'. We know the artist had difficulty finding models – when, that is, he had money to pay them. In the winter this was a bit easier, since agriculture came to a halt. During this period Van Gogh worked with intense pleasure: 'those heads of local women with their white hats – it's difficult, but so incredibly beautiful. They're precisely *clair-obscur* – the white and part of the face in shadow are of such a fine tone'.

The picture of a woman painted in March 1885 is not only the most beautiful in Van Gogh's series of peasant studies, but also one of the few heads he deemed worthy of his signature. The following April he wrote his brother that he had made a pendant for it. Apparently he felt the series came close enough to his ideal – the 'Heads of the People' in *The Graphic* – to qualify as autonomous works. 'Indeed it's difficult to say where a study ends and a painting begins'. The model, Gordina de Groot, figures prominently in Van Gogh's *The Potato Eaters*. She was nearly thirty at the time.

Vincent van Gogh
Head of a Peasant Woman with White Cap
Canvas, 43 × 33.5 cm - March 1885
Inv. S 139 V/1962 - F 130

Vincent van Gogh
Head of a Peasant Woman with White Cap
Canvas, 42 × 34 cm - December 1884
Inv. S 72 V/1962 - F 156

Vincent van Gogh
Head of a Young Peasant with Pipe
Canvas, 38 × 30 cm - winter 1884/85
Inv. S 69 V/1962 - F 164

Vincent van Gogh
Head of a Peasant Woman
Canvas, 43.5 × 30 cm - March/April 1885
Inv. S 84 V/1962 - F 69

Vincent van Gogh
Head of a Peasant Woman with Red Bonnet
Canvas, 43 × 30 cm - April 1885
Inv. S 06 V/1962 - F 160

Vincent van Gogh
Head of a Peasant Woman
Canvas, 42 × 34 cm - April 1885
Inv. S 97 V/1962 - F 269 recto

Vincent van Gogh
Head of a Peasant Woman with White Cap
Canvas, 43.5 × 35.5 cm - May 1885
Inv. S 04 V/1962 - F 388 recto

The Potato Eaters is undoubtedly the most important work Van Gogh produced in Nuenen. With this canvas he realised his long-cherished dream of creating a figure piece in the peasant genre that measured up to his hero Millet. He may have become interested in the motif as early as 1882, when he saw a picture at the Hague branch of Goupil's showing a peasant family at table by Jozef Israëls. Treatments of similar motifs by such artists as Charles de Groux and Léon Lhermitte may have also inspired him. Only after drawing and painting numerous studies of peasant heads in Nuenen did Van Gogh feel up to the challenge, and in the course of 1885 the work began to take shape.

At first he could not decide whether the lighting should be natural or artificial, but finally settled on the latter. An oil study from February/March with four peasants round a table already approximates the definitive composition. On about 11 April 1885 Vincent wrote his brother that he had made a large oil sketch on canvas which in his estimation had 'some life to it'. That same month the Eindhoven lithographer Dimmen Gestel helped him make a litho of the composition, which constitutes an interesting intermediary stage in the evolution of the work. Van Gogh based the litho on the painted study now in the Rijksmuseum Kröller-Müller. He apparently intended to use the litho to solicit reactions to the projected painting from friends and colleagues, and even toyed with the idea of publishing it in the Parisian magazine *Le chat noir*. In the event his friend Anthon van Rappard's reaction was so critical that it effectively ended their relationship.

Ultimately – following 'a tremendous struggle' – Van Gogh painted the definitive picture from memory. The working method was inspired by Delacroix, the dark palette by Israëls and Millet. Théophile Gautier's evocative description of Millet's *Sower* – showing 'peasants painted with the earth they work' – is clearly echoed by the results. Vincent himself said he was trying to achieve the effect 'of a good dusty potato, unpeeled of course'. Even after his style had long since taken a very different direction under the influence of French Impressionism, he still considered *The Potato Eaters* '*après tout* the best [...] I've done'.

Vincent van Gogh
Four Peasants at Table
Canvas, 33 × 41 cm - February/March 1885
Inv. S 135 V/1962 - F 77

Vincent van Gogh
The Potato Eaters
Litho, 36.5 × 32 cm - April 1885
Inv. P 16 V/1962 - F 1661

Vincent van Gogh
The Potato Eaters
Canvas, 82 × 114 cm - April 1885
Inv. S 05 V/1962 - F 82

'What I've tried to do is convey the idea that those people, eating their potatoes by lamplight, have dug the earth with the very hands they put into their bowls. Thus it's about *manual labour*, and about the fact that they've *earned* their food so honestly. I wanted it to make people think about an entirely different way of life than that of us civilised people. So I'm not at all concerned whether everyone likes it straight away or not. All winter long I've had the threads of this tissue in my hands, and have searched for the ultimate pattern; and if it's a tissue that appears rough or coarse, at least the threads have been chosen carefully and in accordance with certain rules. And it might prove to be a *true peasant picture. I know that's what it is.* But if someone prefers a sentimental view of peasants, they're welcome to it. As for myself, I'm convinced you get better results by painting them in their roughness than by bringing conventional charm into it'. (Vincent to Theo, ca. 20 April 1885)

Vincent van Gogh
The Cottage
Canvas, 65.6 × 79 cm - May 1885
Inv. S 87 V/1962 - F 83

In May 1885 Van Gogh finished two important pictures which, together with *The Potato Eaters*, amount to a triptych of rural life. Around the eleventh of the month he wrote his brother about 'a large study of a cottage at dusk' he was working on, and a painting of the old church tower that was about to be pulled down – indeed the spire was 'already gone'. In early June Vincent sent *The Cottage* to Theo in Paris, and the *Country Churchyard with Old Church Tower* shortly thereafter. To underscore the autonomy of both works, he assigned

formal French titles to them: *La chaumière* and *Cimetière de Paysans*. Van Gogh became interested in cottages with thatched roofs while living in Drenthe. His pictures of them recall a canvas by the Barbizon painter Jules Dupré 'with two cottages, their thatched roofs of a surprisingly deep tone against a hazy, dusty evening sky'. He thought of these cottages as 'human nests'; more specifically, they reminded him of a wren's nest, like that he had just found. Vincent's fascination with the Nuenen churchyard can be traced back to

September 1882, while he was still living in The Hague. 'I can't stop thinking about that churchyard with those old crosses. I really hope I'll get around to doing it in due time'. At that point he was planning to paint a peasant funeral in the snow, and before leaving Drenthe had already sketched a simple churchyard he stumbled upon in the midst of the moors. In early June 1885 Van Gogh explained the significance of the *Country Church-yard with Old Church Tower* to his brother. 'I wanted to express how the ruins show that *for centuries* peasants

have been laid to rest there in the very
fields they worked – I wanted to show
how utterly simple death and burial are,
as nice as the falling of the autumn
leaves – just some earth dug up, a
wooden cross. The surrounding fields –
they make a final line against the
horizon above the wall where the grass
of the graveyard ends, like a horizon at
sea. That ruin tells me how a creed and
a religion have mouldered away, even
though they were well established –
how nevertheless the life and death of
the peasants is always the same:

constantly sprouting and withering like
the grass and the flowers growing there
in the churchyard. "Les religions
passent, Dieu demeure," as Victor Hugo
put it, whom they've just buried'. Van
Gogh's critical attitude toward religion
is doubtless related to his difficult
relationship with his father, who had
died recently and been buried in this
very churchyard.
In St-Rémy in April 1890 Van Gogh
considered making new versions of
both pictures. Though he never did so,
several months later he sent his sister a

description of the picture he was
painting of the Auvers village church –
which shows just how much he still had
his Nuenen work in mind. 'Again the
[theme] is almost identical to the studies
of the old tower and the churchyard I
made in Nuenen', he wrote. 'Only now
the colour is probably more expressive,
fuller'.

Vincent van Gogh
Basket with Potatoes
Canvas, 44.5 × 60 cm - September 1885
Inv. S 153 V/1962 - F 100

These still lifes can be dated on the basis of a letter Vincent wrote Theo in late September 1885, explaining the four canvases he had just sent. 'What I have for you are some still lifes – a basket of potatoes, fruit, a copper kettle, etc. – which are really about modelling with various colours'. Félix Bracquemond's book *Du dessin et de la couleur* had got him interested in using colour this way. After sending the works to Theo in Paris, Vincent elaborated on how he had employed colour in the four works. The potato still lifes were conceived as variations on the theme of brownish grey. In a still life with apples, he contrasted not only the complementary colours green and red, but also the fore- and backgrounds. 'I gave the one a natural colour by breaking blue with orange, and the other the same natural colour, except that I altered it by adding some yellow'. Many will find these still lifes unattractive, and indeed it is impossible to understand them without knowing something about the artist's colour experiments. When the painter Achille Cesbron dared to exhibit a still life with potatoes at the Paris Salon in 1888 he was promptly attacked by the critic Henry Houssaye: 'Mr Cesbron [...] offers us adorable potatoes in their jackets. O sancta simplicitas!' Van Gogh had no illusions about the commercial value of potato still lifes; they were strictly studies as far as he was concerned. Self-effacing as always, he concluded the previously quoted letter to his brother with a request: 'And if you find some book or other about colour, send it to me, would you? There's so much more I have to learn, and I try to learn more every day'.

Vincent van Gogh
Basket with Potatoes
Canvas, 50.5 × 66 cm - September 1885
Inv. S 152 V/1962 - F 116

Vincent van Gogh
Basket with Potatoes
Canvas, 33 × 43.5 cm - September 1885
Inv. S 150 V/1962 - F 101

Vincent van Gogh
Still Life with Vegetables and Fruit
Canvas, 32.5 × 43 cm - September 1884
Inv. S 70 V/1962 - F 103

Vincent van Gogh
Still Life with Copper Kettle, Jug and Potatoes
Canvas, 65.5 × 80.5 cm - September 1885
Inv. S 52 V/1962 - F 51

Vincent van Gogh
Two Bird's Nests
Canvas, 31.5 × 42.5 cm - September/October 1885. Inv. S 71 V/1962 - F 109 recto

Living in Nuenen Van Gogh developed a passion for collecting bird's nests, a passion he shared with his fellow painter Anthon van Rappard. Indeed he sent his friend a basket of them in September 1885. 'I too have some in my studio, quite a collection in fact, so I'm sending you some duplicates. They're of thrush, blackbird, golden oriole, wren and finch'. For Van Gogh, skilful nest builders 'such as wrens or golden orioles can surely be considered artists. At the same time [their nests] make beautiful still lifes'.

In early October Vincent wrote his brother that he had painted four still lifes, inspired by his collection of bird's nests. 'I think the colours of the moss, dry leaves and grasses, clay, etc. might appeal to people who know a good deal about nature. [...] Toward winter, if I have more time, I'll make some drawings of this sort of thing. *La nichée et les nids*, that's what I like – especially those *human* nests, those cottages on the heath and their inhabitants'.

The nests, too, were colour studies first of all. Some of them are intentionally cast against a black background so as to indicate 'that the objects appear not in their natural surroundings, but against a conventional *fond*'. Though it was during that very period that he admired the coloured backgrounds of some still lifes in the Rijksmuseum, he decided against them in the end. 'A *living* nest in nature is something else altogether. One hardly sees the nest itself, one sees the birds. But since I want to paint nests *from my own nest collection*, I can't make it clear enough that the background is very different from the natural surroundings. I simply made the background black'.

Vincent van Gogh
Five Bird's Nests
Canvas, 39.5 × 46 cm - September/October 1885 Inv. S 01 V/1962 - F 111

During the second week of October 1885 Van Gogh spent three days in Amsterdam so he could visit the recently opened Rijksmuseum and the Fodor Collection. He took the opportunity to study seventeenth-century masters as well as the work of such contemporary artists as Jozef Israëls. Despite the brevity of his Amsterdam sojourn, he still found time to paint. 'The two small panels I painted in Amsterdam were done in great haste, one even in the waitingroom of the station [...], the other in the morning, before I went to the museum at about ten o'clock'.

This view of several tugs moored behind Amsterdam's railway station was probably the second of these 'small panels'. Vincent was so pleased with his 'little tiles, on which I just threw something down with a few strokes', that he sent them on to Theo, even though they were slightly damaged: 'they got wet en route, then the panels warped while drying, dust got into them, and so forth'.

He wanted to show his brother 'that if I want to spend an hour somewhere tossing off an impression I can just about do so, the same way others analyse their impressions and arrive at an understanding of what they see. That's something other than feeling, that's experiencing impressions – there may be a big difference between experiencing impressions and analysing them, that is *taking them apart and putting them back together again*. It's quite pleasant to throw

Vincent van Gogh
Street in Eindhoven in the Rain
Watercolour, 20.9 × 29.5 cm - November 1885
Inv. D 47 V/1969 - F 1348

something down on the run'.

Van Gogh visited Amsterdam together with Anton Kerssemakers from Eindhoven, to whom he was giving painting lessons at that time. The watercolour of a rainy scene, which he inscribed 'Un dimanche à Eindhoven', is the same sort of rapid, evocative impression as that Vincent painted in Amsterdam.

Vincent van Gogh
The Ruijterkade in Amsterdam with Tugboats
Panel, 20.5 × 27 cm - October 1885
Inv. S 85 V/1962 - F 211

Studying the masters of Holland's Golden Age in the Rijksmuseum reassured Van Gogh that his illustrious precursors would approve of his tonal manner. As he wrote his brother, who had advised him against using black, in October 1885, 'Rembrandt and Hals didn't use black? Or Velàzquez? Not only one, but twenty-seven blacks, I can assure you'. With that Theo qualified his position, citing the black in Manet's picture of a dead toreador (now in Washington's National Gallery of Art). To end the discussion Vincent painted the *Still Life with Bible, Extinguished Candle and Novel*. 'In reply to your description of the Manet study, I'm sending you a still life with an open (and therefore off-white) leatherbound Bible against a black background. The foreground is yellowish brown with a touch of lemon yellow. I painted it *all at once*, in one day'. Two of the three objects in this canvas – the open Bible and the extinguished candle – link it to the time-honoured tradition of the vanitas still life. The text can be identified as Isaiah 53, which proclaims the coming of the servant of the Lord, who shall be despised and rejected of men.

Besides the painterly dialogue with Manet, the still life also has a third dimension.

The Bible can be seen as an allusion to Vincent's father, Rev. Theodorus van Gogh, who died that year. The muted tones of the book, signifying his father's strict piety, contrast with the 'touch of lemon yellow' on the cover of the novel, *La joie de vivre* by the French Naturalist Emile Zola.

There has been a great deal of speculation about the meaning of the worn-out shoes, a theme Van Gogh returned to repeatedly over the years. Even such eminent thinkers as Heidegger and Derrida have tried their hand at them.

The artist's original intent is still uncertain, as is the date. While the canvas is usually assigned to the artist's Parisian period, some would argue it has more in common with his Nuenen work. In January 1894, in an article entitled 'Nature mortes', Paul Gauguin described just such a still life with shoes, which he associated with the artist's departure from Nuenen: 'In my small yellow room, a still life, this time violet. – Two enormous shoes, worn out, misshapen. Vincent's shoes. The pair he put on one morning when they were still new in order to hike from Holland to Belgium'.

Vincent van Gogh
A Pair of Shoes
Canvas, 37.5 × 45 cm - 1885/86
Inv. S 11 V/1962 - F 255

No sooner had Van Gogh arrived in Antwerp on 24 November 1885 than he set out to explore the city and its museums, paying particular attention to the work of Rubens. Here too, however, he found his greatest inspiration on the street: ordinary people who lived and worked in the Scheldt city. 'I see the people on the street – good, but I often find the maidservants so much more interesting and beautiful than the ladies – the labourers more interesting than the gentlemen. And in those ordinary young people I find a strength and vitality one would have to paint with a firm touch, a simple technique, in order to capture their singular character'. And before long he decided it was 'true on the whole what they say about Antwerp, the women are indeed beautiful'.
In early December 1885 Van Gogh painted the heads of a young woman and an old man 'as portrait trials'. He

was very taken with the 'splendid old man' he had found as a model, whose features reminded him of the writer Victor Hugo. The woman's countenance he rendered in light tones, 'white tinted with carmine, vermillion, yellow and a light background of greyish yellow, from which the face is only distinguished by the black hair. Lilac tones in the clothes'. Van Gogh hoped his female heads would sell, but when they failed to do so, he began painting views of the city as tourist souvenirs. 'Yet I prefer painting people's eyes to cathedrals, for however solemn and imposing it may be, there's something in their eyes the cathedral lacks, namely the human soul'.

The curious little canvas with a skeleton smoking is thought to be a joke Van Gogh made while studying at the Antwerp academy.

Vincent van Gogh
Head of a Woman with her Hair Loose
Canvas, 35 × 24 cm - December 1885
Inv. S 59 V/1962 - F 206

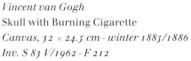

Vincent van Gogh
Skull with Burning Cigarette
Canvas, 32 × 24.5 cm - winter 1885/1886
Inv. S 83 V/1962 - F 212

Vincent van Gogh
Head of an Old Man
Canvas, 44.5 × 33.5 cm
- December 1885
Inv. S 61 V/1962 -
F 205

The intimate view of houses in the snow is one of the first oil studies Vincent made in Antwerp.

As he would later do in Paris he painted it from the window of his flat, located above a paint dealer on Rue des Images.

Vincent van Gogh
Backs of Houses in
Antwerp in the Snow
Canvas, 44 × 33.5 cm -
December 1885
Inv. S 142 V/1962

The Van Gogh Museum preserves practically everything Van Gogh is known to have produced during the three months he spent in Antwerp. A number of the drawings apparently derive from sketchbooks. This is true of the three dance hall scenes, for instance, which are all of virtually the same size; only a few drawings from the sketchbook they belonged to are still known. In a letter to Theo of about 6-7 December 1885, Vincent described a visit to a hall like that in the illustrated sheet: 'Yesterday I was in the café-concert Scala, which is something like the Folies Bergères. I found it very dull and of course insipid, but the audience amused me. There were splendid women's heads, really extraordinarily beautiful, among the good burghers in the seats at the back [...]'.

In his search for models in the Flemish city Van Gogh was repeatedly struck by extremes. One moment he noticed a group of brawny sailors eating mussels, the next 'a Chinese girl, mysterious and quiet as a mouse, small, like a bedbug [...]. Now one sees a girl who is splendidly healthy and at least seems to be very loyal and naïvely gay, then again a face so sly and false that it frightens one, as a hyena would. Not to mention the faces scarred by smallpox, the colour of boiled shrimp, with pale grey eyes, without eyebrows, and thin, sleek hair the colour of real pig bristles or a bit yellower – Swedish or Danish types'.

Vincent van Gogh
Dancing Women
Black and coloured chalk on vellum paper
9.2 × 16.4 cm - December 1885
Inv. D 27 V/1962 - F 1350b

_____

Vincent van Gogh
Two Women in a Loge
Black and coloured chalk on vellum paper
9.5 × 16.5 cm - December 1885
Inv. D 25 V/1962 - F 1350v

_____

Vincent van Gogh
Dance Hall
Black and coloured chalk on vellum paper
9.2 × 16.3 cm - December 1885
Inv. D 26 V/1962 - F 1350a

Vincent van Gogh
Portrait of a Woman
Black and coloured chalk on vellum paper
50.7 × 39.4 cm - winter 1885/86
Inv. D 58 V/1962 - F 1357

Van Gogh in Paris

Fragment of a letter from Van Gogh, written in Paris between August and October 1886, to the English painter Horace M. Livens, whom he had met in Antwerp.

'[...] I intend remaining here still longer. There is much to be seen here – for instance Delacroix, to name only one master. In Antwerp I did not even know what the impressionists were, now I have seen them and though *not* being one of the club yet I have much admired certain impressionists' pictures – *Degas* nude figure – *Claude Monet* landscape. 'And now for what regards what I myself have been doing, I have lacked money for paying models else I had entirely given myself to figure painting. But I have made a series of colour studies in painting simply flowers [...]. 'Now after these gymnastics I lately did two heads which I dare say are better in light and colour than those I did before. So as we said at the time: in *colour* seeking *life* the true drawing is modelling with colour. I did a dozen landscapes too, frankly *green*, frankly *blue*. And so I am struggling for life and progress in art [...].

'As regards my chances of selling, look, they're certainly not great but still *I have made* a beginning. At present I've found four dealers who've exhibited studies of mine, and I've exchanged studies with many artists. [...] I was in Cormon's studio for three or four months but didn't find that as useful as I'd expected it to be. But that may be my fault. Anyhow I left there too, just as I left Antwerp. Since then I've been working alone and fancy that I feel more like myself'.

In early March 1886 Van Gogh had gone to Paris unexpectedly to study in Fernand Cormon's atelier. His Parisian sojourn lasted exactly two years and effectively transformed his work. By the time he left he had become acquainted with both Impressionism and Neo-impressionism. Through his brother Theo, with whom he lodged, he made numerous contacts in the art world. His friendship with Anquetin, Bernard, Signac and Toulouse-Lautrec gave him access to the avant-garde.

Vincent van Gogh
Plaster Torso and Notes
Blue and black chalk on sketchbook sheet
20.3 × 13 cm - 1886
Inv. D 140 V/1962 - FSD 1716 r

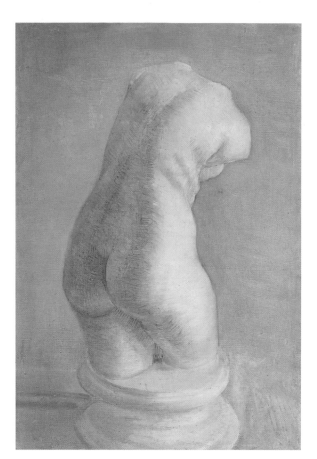

Vincent van Gogh
Plaster Statuette of a Female Torso
Pasteboard, 46 × 38 cm
Inv. S 56 V/1962 - F 216a

—————————

Vincent van Gogh
Plaster Cast of a Torso
Pasteboard, 46.5 × 38 cm
Inv. S 89 V/1962 - F 216b

Vincent van Gogh
Plaster Cast of a Torso
Canvas, 40.5 × 27 cm
Inv. S 199 V/1962 - F 216g

—————————

Vincent van Gogh
Plaster Cast of a Torso
Pasteboard, 32.5 × 24 cm
Inv. S 75 V/1963 - F 216i

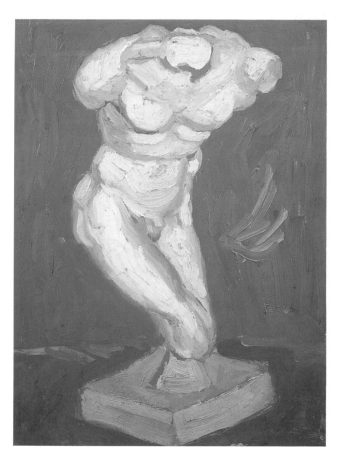

Vincent van Gogh
Plaster Cast of a
Kneeling Man
Pasteboard, 35 × 27 cm
Inv. S 102 V/1962 - F 216f

Vincent van Gogh
Plaster Cast of a Torso
Pasteboard, 35 × 27 cm
Inv. S 103 V/1962 - F 216e

Vincent van Gogh
Plaster Cast of a Horse
Pasteboard, 33 × 41 cm
Inv. S 202 V/1962 - F 216c

One of Van Gogh's motives for going to Paris was to pursue his artistic training in Fernand Cormon's atelier. Though the exact dates of his attendance are not known, he presumably reported soon after his arrival in the French capital, and spent a total of three or four months. Most of the time he worked from live models or plaster casts. Besides countless study drawings, he also produced an attractive series of oil studies after plaster casts against a blue background. Several of the original casts are preserved in the Museum. Cormon's studio proved to be a breeding ground for the avant-garde. It was there that Van Gogh met Emile Bernard, Louis Anquetin, Henri de Toulouse-Lautrec and the Australian Impressionist John Russell, for instance.

Vincent van Gogh
Self-portrait with Dark Felt Hat
Canvas, 41.5 × 32.5 cm - 1886
Inv. S 162 V/1962 - F 208a

Of the many self-portraits Van Gogh painted, no less than eighteen of which are in the Van Gogh Museum, most date from his Parisian period.

It was in Antwerp that he decided to become a portraitist. Like Rembrandt early in his career, he turned to self-portraiture as an inexpensive method of studying the effects of light.

The three self-portraits illustrated here are among the earliest Vincent is known to have painted in Paris. As yet there seems to be no trace of the profound self-analysis many have read into these canvases. They are still distinguished by the dark palette of his Nuenen period and a Rembrandtesque incidence of light. In his dress, however, we see him break new ground: whereas in Brabant he had usually worn a peasant blouse, here he sports a felt hat apparently in an attempt to identify himself as a city dweller.

Living with his brother, he must have felt a certain obligation to adapt to Theo's circle of friends, and indeed Archibald S. Hartrick, with whom Vincent studied in Paris, recalled in *A Painter's Pilgrimage through Fifty Years* that he 'dressed quite well and in an ordinary way, better than many in the atelier'. The two self-portraits with the pipe seem somewhat later than that with the felt hat.

Vincent van Gogh
The Hill of Montmartre with Quarry
Canvas, 56.2 × 62.5 cm - 1886
Inv. S 12 V/1962 - F 230

Vincent van Gogh
Sloping Path on Montmartre
Pasteboard, 22 × 16 cm - 1886
Inv. S 92 V/1963 - F 232

Vincent van Gogh
Factories Seen from a Hillside
Canvas, 21 × 46.5 cm - 1887
Inv. S 133 M/1970 - F 266a

Montmartre had long been popular with artists. In Hendrik Willem Mesdag's collection in The Hague, Van Gogh had had the opportunity to admire two pictures with windmills in the suburb by Georges Michel (1763-1843), and he himself owned a print with Montmartre subjects by August Delâtre, which probably influenced his choice of themes. Van Gogh made the fresh outdoor study of the quarry in the autumn of 1886. His fellow countryman Matthijs Maris had previously painted it in the early 1870s (Gemeentemuseum, The Hague). Though the windmill just to the right of centre plays a relatively minor role within the composition, its placement at the intersection of the dramatic bank of clouds and the fence running diagonally over the hill focuses our attention on it. The Blute-Fin, as the mill was called, formed the subject of many other pictures Van Gogh painted during this period.

In June 1886 Vincent and Theo van Gogh moved into a flat in Rue Lepic, located on the Butte Montmartre. During his first stay in Paris in 1875/76 Van Gogh had lived in the same quarter. This period witnessed the suburb's gradual absorption by the burgeoning metropolis and its hey-day as a centre of entertainment. Despite these changes, Montmartre retained some of its rural charm, which fascinated Vincent, even if he occasionally included the factories in his work.

Vincent van Gogh
View of the Roofs of Paris
Canvas, 54 × 72.5 cm - 1886
Inv. S 13 V/1962 - F 261

The manner of these early Parisian views is still tonal, and more closely related to Corot and the Barbizon School than to the Impressionists. Vincent became acquainted with the latter at this time, but had not yet been converted to their particular vision.

On 10 July 1887 Theo van Gogh wrote his friend Caro van Stockum-Haanebeek in The Hague about the recent changes in his domestic life. 'As you may know I am living with my brother Vincent, who is studying painting with inexhaustible zeal. Since he needs a fair amount of space for his work, we are living in a rather large flat in Montmartre which, as you know, is built against a hill on the outskirts of Paris. The most remarkable thing about it is the splendid view of the city from one of the windows, with the hills of Meudon, St Cloud and so forth on the horizon, and a piece of sky almost as large as when one stands on the dunes. 'With all the effects the changing sky produces, it's a theme for I don't know how many pictures. If you saw it you'd add that it is even suitable for poetry'.

Vincent van Gogh
Vase with Forget-Me-Nots and Peonies
Pasteboard, 34.5 × 27.5 cm - summer 1886
Inv. S 182 V/1962 - F 243a

Vincent van Gogh
Glass with Roses
Pasteboard, 35 × 27 cm - summer 1886
Inv. S 178 V/1962 - F 218

Vincent van Gogh
Coleus in a Flowerpot
Canvas, 42 × 22 cm - summer 1886
Inv. S 185 V/1962 - F 281

The fact that most of the flower still lifes Vincent painted in Paris are unsigned indicates that they were originally colour studies. In late July 1886 Theo wrote their mother that Vincent's friends regularly supplied him with fresh flowers that summer for these 'finger exercises'. In a letter about his first months in Paris to the English painter Horace Mann Livens, whom he had met in Antwerp, Vincent wrote: 'I have lacked money for paying models else I had entirely given myself to figure painting. But I have made a series of colour studies in painting, simply flowers, red poppies, blue corn flowers and forget-me-nots, white and pink roses, yellow chrysanthemums – looking for contrasts between blue and orange, red and green, yellow and violet for *les tons rompus et neutres* to harmonise brutal extremes. Trying to achieve intense *colour* and not *grey* harmony'.

While living in Brabant Van Gogh immersed himself in colour theory by reading Charles Blanc's *Grammaire des arts du dessin*. Though he had previously painted a few flower still lifes in Nuenen, in Paris he had the opportunity to test his theoretical knowledge against the practice of other still-life painters. Theo himself owned flower pieces by Jeannin and Fantin-Latour; as well as a watercolour with grapes and pears by Sientje Mesdag-van Houten, these are now in the Van Gogh Museum. At the Salon of 1886, moreover, Vincent admired the work of the flower painter Ernest Quost. But the Provençal painter Adolphe Monticelli, one of whose flower still lifes was in the Van Gogh brothers' collection, had the greatest impact on him by far. In February 1890, after Albert Aurier had praised Van Gogh as 'the only painter who observes colour gradations with that intensity, with that sharpness of metal and precious stones', Vincent modestly referred the critic to this picture in Theo's collection, 'a certain bouquet by Monticelli – a bouquet in white, forget-me-not blue and orange'.

Van Gogh's impasto is often traced to Monticelli. Yet these still lifes also recall a painting by Manet that Vincent and Theo had seen at the Parisian auction house of Drouot: a bouquet of 'large pink peonies with their green leaves against a light background', painted 'in thick impastos and not built up from layers of transparent paint, like those of Jeannin'. The work by Manet seems to have inspired many a flower piece by Van Gogh.

The still life *Mussels and Shrimps* calls to mind a rather pathetic anecdote in Gauguin's posthumously published *Avant et Après*. The Frenchman recounts how, in the winter of 1886, a numb and hungry Van Gogh walked into a junk shop on Rue Lepic to sell 'a small still life – pink shrimps on a pink background', so that he could buy food. 'Poor artist!' wrote Gauguin. 'You've invested part of your soul in the small canvas you've come to sell'. No sooner had the dealer given him 100 sous for it, than the impecunious painter handed the money to a beggar who chanced to pass at that moment.

Vincent van Gogh
Mussels and Shrimps
Canvas, 26.5 × 34.5 cm - autumn 1886
Inv. S 122 V/1962 - F 256

Vincent van Gogh
Vase with Asters and Phlox
Canvas, 61 × 46 cm - summer 1886
Inv. S 177 V/1962 - F 234

Vincent van Gogh
Vase with Gladioli
Canvas, 46.5 × 38.5 cm - summer 1886
Inv. S 144 V/1962 - F 248a

Vincent van Gogh
Boulevard de Clichy, Paris
Pen, ink and pastel on paper,
38 × 52.5 cm - 1887
Inv. D 356 V/1962 - F 1393

Vincent recorded this view of Boulevard de Clichy from Place Blanche, a few steps from the flat where he and Theo lived in Rue Lepic. The Boulevard figured prominently in the life of the Impressionists: it was there that Toulouse-Lautrec's Moulin Rouge and Vincent's Café du Tambourin were located, that Cormon had his atelier, and that Frank Boggs, John Russell, Georges Seurat and Paul Signac lived. Though Impressionists of the previous generation such as Degas and Renoir also resided there, Van Gogh associated the neighbourhood with the younger generation, whom he dubbed the 'Impressionnistes du Petit Boulevard'. In this animated cityscape the Dutch artist focused for the first time on Parisian street life, which Impressionists such as Monet and Pissarro had previously treated with verve. The view in both drawing and painting is virtually the same, even if it is more

Vincent van Gogh
Boulevard de Clichy, Paris
Canvas, 46.5 × 55 cm - 1887
Inv. S 94 V/1962 - F 292

concentrated in the painted version and
seen at closer range.

The similarities between them
notwithstanding, there are some
striking differences as well. The sense
of depth is much more pronounced in
the drawing, for instance, thanks in
particular to the figures in the
foreground which do not recur in the
painting.

The colours in the sheet are less
distinct, and the predominance of blue
tints accounts for the relative coolness
of the light. Finally in the painting, the
artist's impressionistic manner enabled
him to achieve a sunnier, more even
effect. The naked trees suggest that
both date from February-March 1887.

Vincent van Gogh
View from Vincent's Room on Rue Lepic
Canvas, 46 × 38 cm - 1887
Inv. S 57 V/1962 - F 341

Vincent van Gogh
A Corner of Montmartre
Canvas, 34.5 × 64.5 cm - 1887
Inv. S 14 V/1962 - F 347

———————

———————

Vincent van Gogh
Vegétable Gardens and the Moulin de Blute-Fin
on Montmartre
Canvas, 44.8 × 81 cm - 1887
Inv. S 15 V/1962 - F 346

These three works from the spring of 1887 show how Van Gogh's palette became more colourful following his exposure to Impressionism, and how he was also influenced by the stippling of the Neo-impressionists. Remarkably enough, he would sometimes combine these styles in his own idiosyncratic fashion in the same painting.

In his depiction of the vegetable gardens Van Gogh pretended that Montmartre had retained its rural character. Yet the charming canvas with figures strolling past the windmills leaves no doubt that, with its superb view, Montmartre was in fact fast becoming a popular destination for Parisians looking to escape the city for a day.

Vincent van Gogh
Self-portrait
Pasteboard, 19 × 14 cm - 1887
Inv. S 155 V/1962 - F 267

Vincent van Gogh
Self-portrait with Straw Hat
Pasteboard, 19 × 14 cm - 1887
Inv. S 157 V/1962 - F 294

If we compare these self-portraits to the first ones Van Gogh painted in Paris, we can see how far his use of colour had evolved in the course of a year. The browns of Nuenen gave way to blues, reds, greens, yellows and pinks. The brushwork also became more distinctive.

That Vincent felt comfortable in the rather elegant clothes he is wearing in these small works – none of which measures more than 19 by 14 centimetres – seems rather unlikely. He may have meant to dress according to contemporary bourgeois taste in order to practice the sort of formal portraiture

Vincent van Gogh
Self-portrait with Grey Felt Hat
Pasteboard, 19 × 14 cm - 1887
Inv. S 156 V/1962 - F 296

with which he hoped to earn a living someday.

The portrait of the young woman shows just how far Van Gogh had got on the road to becoming a portraitist. On 28 February 1887 his brother wrote their mother in Holland that 'Vincent has painted some portraits that have turned out well, but he never charges anything for them'. Though *Woman by a Cradle* is usually dated somewhat later – to the spring of 1887 – Theo could possibly have had this portrait in mind. Vincent may have borrowed the motif from female colleagues such as Berthe Morisot and Mary Cassatt, whose pictures in this vein he must have known. As regards technique, the canvas lies somewhere between Impressionism and Neo-impressionism, not unlike Toulouse-Lautrec's *Young Woman at a Table (Poudre de riz)* in the Van Gogh Museum.

The woman who sat for this portrait was identified several years ago. She is Léonie-Rose Davy, a niece of the art dealer Pierre-Firmin Martin, who married the tradesman Charles-Nicolas Charbuy. 'Père' Martin, as he was called, was a colleague and friend of Theo van Gogh. He dealt in such Impressionists as Guillaumin, Pissarro and Sisley and also had several of Vincent's works in stock. Given the pictures hanging on the wall behind her, Léonie-Rose probably sat for the portrait in the flat of the art dealer at N° 29 Rue St-Georges, where she herself had been living since 1883. As Martin's only heir, the young woman carried on his business after he died in 1891.

Vincent van Gogh
Woman Sitting by a Cradle
Canvas, 61 × 45.5 cm - 1887
Inv. S 165 V/1962 - F 369

Vincent van Gogh
A Pair of Shoes
Pasteboard, 33 × 41 cm - 1887
Inv. S 127 V/1962 - F 331

Vincent van Gogh
Still Life with Pansies
Canvas, 46 × 55.5 cm - 1886
Inv. S 180 V/1962 - F 244

The motif of a woman at a table, be she of questionable character or not, had been popular with Impressionists ever since Degas painted his famous *Absinthe Drinker*. Manet and Toulouse-Lautrec each treated the theme several times. The woman smoking a cigarette with the remarkable headdress, whom Van Gogh showed sitting at this tambourine-shaped table, is the proprietress of Café du Tambourin on Boulevard de Clichy. Of Italian origins, her name was Agostina Segatori. She had modelled regularly for painters in the 1860s, including Corot and Gérôme. Though Vincent seems to have been more than a friend to Segatori, who has evidently aged somewhat in the meantime, we know very little about their relationship – until, that is, they fell out at the end of the summer of 1887. Bernard tells us that Van Gogh used to pay for his board with flowers 'that last forever' – still lifes, in other words – which were used to decorate the café. The fact that the Pansies rest on a tambourine-shaped table would seem to indicate that he painted them in her establishment. We know from his correspondence that Van Gogh had been irritated by cafés without pictures while he was still living in Antwerp, and planned to remedy the situation with portraits and still lifes. Perhaps he got 'La Segatori' to see eye to eye.

It was in the Café du Tambourin that Van Gogh organised an exhibition of Japanese prints which – he claimed – would profoundly influence his Parisian colleagues Bernard and Anquetin. The portrait of Segatori makes reference to this exhibition. Not only is a Japanese painting or print indicated in the right background, but also other elements, such as the parasol, point to Japan. The still life with a pair of shoes likewise dates from the first half of 1887. Though there were precedents – such as pictures by the Realists François Bonvin and Théodule Ribot – shoes are a theme that has always been associated with Van Gogh. Indeed the Dutch artist's very first oil painting featured a pair of wooden clogs. Many have interpreted the motif as a symbol of the suffering with which his life was fraught. According to the Parisian painter François Gauzi, who studied in Cormon's atelier together with Van Gogh, his comrades found his subject matter somewhat bizarre. Yet it could not really be called revolutionary: Thomas Couture was already painting worn-out footwear in 1865, as though it were part of the stock-in-trade of any self-respecting Realist.

Vincent van Gogh
Woman in Café Le Tambourin
Canvas, 55.5 × 46.5 cm - 1887
Inv. S 17 V/1962 - F 370

In all their simplicity these three works are clearly distinguished from the early still lifes Van Gogh painted as colour studies in Paris. The lighter palette makes a far more modern impression, and the contrast between each of the objects and the pattern in the background shows how much the artist had learned from Japanese prints. In Arles, Vincent would take this decorative approach one step further, as seen for instance in the background of his portraits of the postman Roulin and his wife the 'Berceuse'.
The fact that the stripes in the background of the two illustrated pictures are vertical while they are horizontal in one of the artist's other still lifes suggests that they are not modelled on the wallpaper in Van Gogh's flat, but on a piece of loose paper or fabric he used as a backdrop. If the application of the paint is any indication, Vincent did not spend much time on the still life with lemons. Despite the speed at which he was working, he convincingly described the light reflecting on the glass carafe. At the same time he demonstrated his knowledge of colour theory in the contrasts between the complementary colours yellow and purple in the plate of lemons, and between the red and green in the fore- and background. He must have been pleased with the results: the still life is one of the few works he not only signed but also dated.

Vincent van Gogh
Flowerpot with Chives
Canvas, 31.5 × 22 cm - spring 1887
Inv. S 183 V/1962 - F 337

Vincent van Gogh
Lemons on a Plate
Canvas, 21 × 26.5 cm - spring 1887
Inv. S 193 V/1962 - F 338

Vincent van Gogh
Lemons on a Plate and a Carafe
Canvas, 46.5 × 38.5 cm - spring 1887
Inv. S 20 V/1962 - F 340

The unusual oval format of these two still lifes corresponds to the shape of the Japanese tea boxes on which they are painted. The basket of germinating crocuses would seem to be a celebration of spring. Van Gogh saw the germinative power of a flower bulb or a grain of wheat as an emblem of human love. This constitutes the thematic link between the basket of flowers painted on the lid of the one box and the three novels on that of the other. The novels were all written by Naturalist authors dear to the artist. They are *Braves gens* by Jean Richepin, *Au bonheur des dames* by Emile Zola and *La fille Elisa* by Edmond de Goncourt. All three are set in contemporary Paris and concern the positive role of women in romantic relationships. Though we have no way of knowing whether this theme had any bearing on the artist's own life at the time, he did confide in his sister that he was 'still constantly [having] the most impossible and implausible love affairs, which I generally come away from with only injury and embarrassment'. As a painterly motif, the books are said to derive from Paul Signac, who is known to have done a very similar still life; yet Van Gogh painted his *Still Life with Bible*, showing Zola's novel *La joie de vivre* in the foreground, even before he left Nuenen.

Vincent van Gogh
Three Novels
Panel, 31 × 48.5 cm - spring 1887
Inv. S 181 V/1962 - F 335

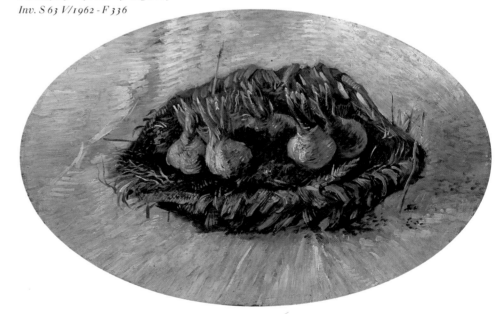

Vincent van Gogh
Basket of Sprouting Flower Bulbs
Panel, 31.5 × 48 cm - spring 1887
Inv. S 63 V/1962 - F 336

The still life with the stack of novels is actually a study for a slightly larger painting that was exhibited at the fourth exhibition of the Société des Artistes Indépendants in 1888. 'Romans parisiens' is also the subtitle of Richepin's *Braves gens*, one of the books seen in the oval still life. Though in contrast to that picture the titles of these books are illegible, they are likely to have been written by such Naturalists as Goncourt, Huysmans, Maupassant, Richepin and Zola, who depicted life 'as we feel it and thus satisfy our need to be told the truth [...] one can scarcely be said to belong to one's own time if one knows nothing about them'.

There has been a good deal of speculation about the date of this canvas. Given the confident touch, some specialists see it as a later variant from Arles. But a recent comparison between the two paintings showed that it was painted in Paris as a study for the definitive version, which was displayed at the Indépendants.

Vincent van Gogh
'Romans parisiens'
Canvas, 53 × 73.2 cm - 1887
Inv. S 21 V/1962 - F 358

Vincent van Gogh
The Ramparts of Paris with Horsetram and
Pedestrians (La Barrière)
Pencil, ink, pastel and watercolour,
39.5 × 53.5 cm - summer 1887
Inv. D 355 V/1962 - F 1400

In the summer of 1887 Van Gogh set out to paint a series of works depicting the fortifications around Paris. A number of his preparatory drawings of the fortifications survive, but to our knowledge he never got as far as transferring any of his ideas to canvas. One of the sketchbooks in the Van Gogh Museum contains several schematic studies of the ramparts. The two elaborately coloured drawings shown here were probably executed in the studio on the basis of them.

When Van Gogh was living in the capital Paris boasted over fifty city gates, constructed between 1841 and 1845. Their demolition commenced in the 1880s, after they had proven ineffective during the Franco-Prussian War of 1870-71. The present drawings show the fortifications around the Porte de Clichy, which the artist passed whenever he went to Asnières to paint. The tall building in the drawing on the right stood on Boulevard Bessières, just east of the Porte de Clichy.

An air of ill repute clung to the walls of Paris. They were flanked by poor neighbourhoods along much of their length, and became the scene of crime and prostitution after dark. In token of the 'terrains vagues' in which they

Vincent van Gogh
The Ramparts of Paris with Horsetram and
Pedestrians (La Barrière)
Pencil, ink and watercolour,
24 × 31.5 cm - summer 1887
Inv. D 420 V/1962 - F 1401

operated, the prostitutes themselves were known as 'terrières' or 'rempardeuses'. The writers Daudet and Huysmans and the illustrators Raffaëlli and Steinlen – all favourites of Van Gogh – had previously recorded the fortifications in word and image, and we may assume he was familiar with at least some of their efforts. The Van Gogh Museum preserves an anonymous engraving from the brothers' collection, moreover, entitled *Escaping Paris by Night*; it shows a group of men surreptitiously lowering themselves from the city walls by moonlight.

But the walls also had happier connotations for Parisians. On Sundays, they would seek out the fortifications to stroll or sit in the sun, as a respite from their daily existence in the dreary industrial zone of Clichy. Steinlen painted a radiant picture of the walls which, like Van Gogh's drawings, must date from around 1887 (Musée cantonal des Beaux-Arts, Lausanne); its palette and composition have much in common with the Dutch artist's handling of the motif.

In the river views Van Gogh created during the summer of 1887 he comes closest to the world of the Impressionists, with whose art he was well acquainted by now. The small view of the Seine, which he probably painted from the Ile des Ravageurs near Asnières, recalls the work of Monet and Sisley.

The influence of Pointillism is equally manifest in the work Van Gogh produced that summer. Indeed he frequently accompanied his friend Paul Signac, one of the style's pioneers, on excursions. Thematically this view of the Pont de la Grande-Jatte heralds that of the Pont de Trinquetaille, which Van Gogh would paint later in Arles.

Vincent van Gogh
The Seine with the Pont de la Grande-Jatte
Canvas, 32 × 40.5 cm - summer 1887
Inv. S 86 V/1962 - F 304

Vincent van Gogh
The Banks of the Seine
Canvas, 32 × 46 cm - summer 1887
Inv. S 77 V/1962 - F 293

Vincent van Gogh
Road along the Seine near Asnières
Canvas, 49 × 65.5 cm - summer 1887
Inv. S 55 V/1962 - F 299

Though there is nothing about the small
figure in this sunny river landscape that
would typify him as a painter, it is nonetheless tempting to identify him with
Vincent van Gogh. We know both from
contemporary descriptions and self-
portraits that a blue workman's smock
and a straw hat were his uniform during
this period.

Vincent van Gogh
Road in a Park at Asnières
Canvas, 33 × 42 cm - 1887
Inv. S 98 V/1963 - F 275

These two paintings of the Voyer d'Argenson park at Asnières show how Van Gogh employed rather divergent techniques in the same period, depending on the purpose of the work at hand. The view on the left is clearly a sketch, painted rapidly *en plein air* without figures.

Figures in a Park at Asnières represents Van Gogh's most ambitious but nonetheless idiosyncratic adaptation of the stippled manner developed by the Neo-impressionists. Rather than uniform dots of paint, he opted for a more expressive variation in the form of small, individual stripes or dashes in

different directions. This enabled him to emphasise the divergent textures of the ground, the shrubbery, the trees and the sky.

Thematically the picture bridges the worlds of Watteau's *fêtes galantes* and the sun-drenched gardens of Monet and Renoir. With this, one of his largest canvases, Van Gogh made his formal Parisian debut: in the winter of 1887-88 it hung alongside work by Seurat and Signac at the Théâtre Libre d'Antoine. Van Gogh's meagre Parisian correspondence makes no mention of the scene in the park, but in a letter from Arles he refers specifically to the

picture as 'the garden with the lovers'.
As regards colour, one of his couples in
a similar painting from Arles
corresponds perfectly with the lovers
seen here in Asnières: 'a couple in love,
the man pale blue wearing a yellow hat,
the upper part of the woman's body
pink'.

With this theme Van Gogh upheld the
tradition that began with Rubens's
Garden of Love (Prado, Madrid), of
which Watteau's *fêtes galantes* was
another highpoint he admired. In the
nineteenth century the *jardin d'amour*
was revived by the painters Diaz and
Monticelli. In a letter of February 1890

to the critic Albert Aurier, Vincent
placed Monticelli on a par with Watteau
as a painter of *fêtes galantes*, and as a
character with Boccaccio. Van Gogh's
description of Monticelli as a
descendant of Boccaccio gives some
idea of how the painter subconsiously
viewed his own garden of love: 'A
melancholic, rather resigned worrier
who sees the festive world of
entertainment, the lovers of his day,
pass him by, and then paints and
analyses them – he, the outcast'.

Vincent van Gogh
Vegetable Gardens on Montmartre
Canvas, 81 × 100 cm - April-June 1887
Inv. S 18 V/1962 - F 316

This view of Montmartre may have originally formed part of a series of landscapes full of 'cheerfulness and fresh air' which the artist considered suitable for decoration and which he mentioned in a letter to his brother in the summer of 1887, while Theo was visiting Holland. Be that as it may, Vincent regarded the large canvas worthy of admission to the Salon des Indépendants in 1888. Later on he thought about presenting it to the museum of modern art in The Hague by way of introducing himself to his countrymen as a full-fledged Impressionist. In response to a review of the Indépendants by Gustave Kahn, claiming that the artist had devoted too little attention to tonal values, Van Gogh argued that it was impossible to paint colour and tone at once: 'You can't be at the pole and at the equator simultaneously. You have to choose, as I hope to do. It will probably end up being colour'.

Vincent van Gogh
Self-portrait with Straw Hat
Canvas, 41 × 31 cm
Inv. S 60 V/1962 - F 61v

Vincent van Gogh
Self-portrait
Canvas, 41 × 33 cm
Inv. S 135 V/1962 - F 77v

Vincent van Gogh
Self-portrait
Canvas, 42.5 × 31.5 cm
Inv. S 71 V/1962 - F 109v

Five of these self-portraits were painted on the backs of canvases Vincent had previously used in Nuenen for studies: heads of peasants, a composition sketch for *The Potato Eaters* and still lifes. The fact that he did not overpaint them suggests that the studies continued to be of some interest to him. They did, after all, form part of a carefully accumulated repertoire the artist thought he might perhaps need at some later date.

Most of these self-portraits have blue backgrounds, were painted in the summer of 1887 and are preoccupied once again with colour and light.

As we can see, Vincent was still his own principal model. Having just successfully completed several more or

Vincent van Gogh
Self-portrait
Canvas, 41.5 × 31.5 cm
Inv. S 68 V/1962 - F 179v

Vincent van Gogh
Self-portrait
Canvas, 42 × 34 cm
Inv. S 97 V/1962 - F 269v

less Pointillist self-portraits, he now experimented with a broader, looser brushstroke and more thinly applied paint.

Compared with the series of small self-portraits he had made in the spring, his approach is now bolder, the result more psychologically charged. This time the painter seems to be as interested in representing different moods as in the technical aspects of his craft. Though they are artistically uneven, the growing self-analys evident in some of these works heralds the penetrating self-portraits of his final years.

Vincent van Gogh
Self-portrait
Canvas, 42 × 30 cm
Inv. S 163 V/1962 - F 524

In a letter to his former fellow student in Antwerp, Horace Mann Livens, Van Gogh wrote from Paris that he had done 'a dozen landscapes, frankly *green*, frankly *blue*'. Though he was probably not referring to these particular studies, they manifest the same determination to explore the infinite nuances of a particular colour. As a theme, forest views were pre-eminently suited to this end. The French term 'sousbois' denotes a closely observed woodland scene that emphasises the ground cover.

Vincent van Gogh
Trees
Canvas, 46.5 × 36 cm - summer 1887
Inv. S 78 V/1963 - F 307

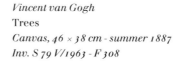

Vincent van Gogh
Path in the Forest
Canvas, 46 × 38.5 cm - summer 1887
Inv. S 80 V/1962 - F 309

Vincent van Gogh
Trees
Canvas, 46 × 38 cm - summer 1887
Inv. S 79 V/1963 - F 308

Vincent van Gogh
Trees
Canvas, 46.5 × 55.5 cm - summer 1887
Inv. S 66 V/1962 - F 309a

Vincent could well have known the motif through the work of one of the Barbizon School painters, Diaz de la Peña, who specialised in the handling of light in forest views.

This closely related group of sylvan scenes from Vincent's Parisian period gave him ample opportunity to experiment with patterns of colour and light in a manner that recalls not only Diaz but also Monticelli and even Seurat. Pains were evidently taken to vary the texture of the paint, while at the same time a sense of depth is clearly suggested.

Ivy's propensity to cover trees and plants was something that always fascinated Van Gogh. Living in London in the mid-1870s he was charmed by the vine, and later, during his stay in Dordrecht in January 1877, he wrote of gazing out of his room 'on gardens with beech and poplar and so forth and the backs of houses [...] overgrown with ivy'. The sight reminded him of a favourite line from Charles Dickens: 'a strange old plant is the ivy green'. Toward the end of his life, while convalescing in the hospital of St-Rémy, Vincent again chose trees overgrown with ivy as the subject of several drawings and paintings.

Vincent van Gogh
Entrance to a Garden on Montmartre
Pencil, ink and watercolour, 31.6 × 24 cm -
summer 1887
Inv. D 148 V/1962 - F 1406

Vincent van Gogh
Barn on Montmartre, with Sunflowers
Pencil, ink and watercolour, 30.5 × 24 cm -
summer 1887
Inv. D 352 V/1962 - F 1411

These pages are filled with images of the summer of 1887: sunny views of Montmartre and the façade of an unidentified edifice. The potted shrubbery and the outdoor table have led some to think the building is a restaurant, but it could just as easily be the house of one of Vincent's painter friends, or perhaps the flat of the countess De la Boissière in Asnières, which according to one of the artist's letters was located above a restaurant. A year later, Vincent's own yellow house in Arles was painted the same colours as the exterior in the illustrated canvas. As he wrote his sister Wil in September 1888, 'The outside of my house here is painted the colour of fresh butter, with bright green shutters, and it gets direct sunlight'.

The coloured drawings represent picturesque corners of what was at that time the still somewhat rustic Butte Montmartre, with its panoramic prospects of Paris. Like the aforementioned picture of the 'restaurant', there is something unmistakeably Japanese about the drawings, which call to mind the artist's passion for Japanese woodcuts. One striking detail is the red, white and blue flag. At first glance it appears to be the French Tricolour, yet on closer inspection the stripes appear to be horizontal, not vertical, making the flag Dutch, not French. Could this be Van Gogh's idea of joke?

In the drawing of a barn with a vegetable garden at the edge of the Butte Montmartre, sunflowers make their first appearance in this volume. They would become the artist's universally recognised trademark.

Vincent van Gogh
Exterior of a Restaurant
Canvas, 18.5 × 27 cm - summer 1887
Inv. S 134 V/1962 - F 321

Vincent van Gogh
Sunflowers
Canvas, 21 × 27 cm - summer 1887
Inv. S 121 V/1963 - F 377

Vincent painted his first sunflowers in
1886, in a still life with other blooms
(Kunsthalle Mannheim). They also
occur in several painted and drawn
Montmartre landscapes of 1887.
The illustrated still life is a study
preparatory to three ambitious pictures.
Two of these were exhibited in the
Restaurant du Chalet in late 1887, and
subsequently exchanged with Gauguin
for other works.

Vincent van Gogh
Wheatfield with Lark
Canvas, 54 × 65.5 cm - summer 1887
Inv. S 197 V/1962 - F 310

Amid the bustle of Paris, which by his own account eventually exhausted him, in the summer of 1887 Van Gogh found occasion to don a straw hat and paint *en plein air*. The straightforward design of the *Wheatfield with Lark* suits the simplicity of the theme. Only the bird, rising out of the windswept wheat, breaches the strict symmetry of the parallel strips of earth, wheat and sky. Thanks to the rich variation between the brushwork in each zone, the canvas seems to quiver with life. In the 1870s Van Gogh was already fond of Michelet's poem 'L'Alouette' (The Lark), and while he was still living in Antwerp, he wrote his brother about what the bird's song meant to him.

'Today, Sunday, it was almost spring. All I did this morning was walk about the entire city [...]. The weather was so beautiful that one could probably hear larks outside for the first time. In short, there was a bit of resurrection in the air'.

Vincent van Gogh
Self-portrait with Straw Hat
Pasteboard, 40.5 × 32.5 cm - summer 1887
Inv. S 164 V/1962

Toward the end of the time he spent in Paris Van Gogh painted several powerful still lifes with fruit. If one compares them with the studies of colour and tone from his Nuenen period, the progress he had made during the previous two years – under the influence of Impressionism – is clearly evident.

In the 1880s Seurat had begun dotting his frames with colours complementary to those in his pictures so as to enhance their effect. Apparently inspired by this, his Dutch colleague also experimented with frames. At times he painted a crimson line on the canvas itself. In the case of the still life dedicated to his brother, at first he applied red paint to the inner (or sight) edge of the frame – until, that is, he changed his mind, and finally painted the entire frame in tones consonant with the picture. The touches of paint on the framework occasionally resemble Japanese ideograms. They are also intended to approximate the crinkly effect of a type of Japanese print known as a 'crepon'. The Van Gogh Museum preserves a Chinese lacquer box containing a number of multi-coloured balls of wool. The artist used these to gauge the effect that various colour combinations would have. One of them perfectly matches the palette of the illustrated still life dedicated to Theo. It is a study not so much of colour contrasts as of closely related tones, in which various shades of yellow and brown are harmonised. Only here and there have a few dots of contrasting colours been applied.

Vincent van Gogh
Apples
Canvas, 46 × 61.5 cm - autumn 1887
Inv. S 131 V/1962 - F 254

Chinese lacquer box with 16 balls of wool
Wood, metal and red lacquer, 29.8 × 10.6 × 15.5 cm
Inv. V 43 V/1962

Vincent van Gogh
White Grapes, Apples, Pears and Lemons
Dedicated 'à mon frère Theo'
Canvas, 48.5 × 65 cm - autumn 1887
Inv. S 23 V/1970 - F 383

Vincent van Gogh
Red Cabbages and Onions
Canvas, 50 × 64.5 cm - autumn 1887
Inv. S 82 V/1963 - F 374

Vincent van Gogh
Japonaiserie: The Blossoming Plum (after Hiroshige)
Canvas, 55 × 46 cm - summer/autumn 1887
Inv. S 115 V/1962 - F 371

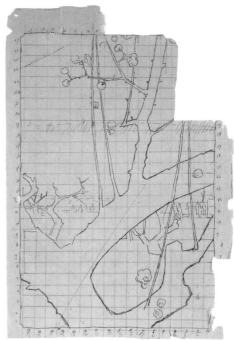

Vincent van Gogh
Tracing of Hiroshige's print
'The Blossoming Plum'
Pencil and ink on transparent paper,
38 × 25.8 cm
Inv. D 772 V/1962

The two paintings shown here, which Vincent modelled on famous compositions by Hiroshige, are among the most unequivocal expressions of his love for Japanese woodcuts, of which he and his brother collected hundreds. Though it is not known exactly when the paintings were made, on the basis of style they are generally dated to the summer or autumn of 1887.
The colours of the canvases are far more intense than those of the original prints. After moving to Arles, where he thought he had found the perfect equivalent of Japan, Van Gogh claimed he no longer needed Japanese prints. It was enough 'to keep my eyes open and paint whatever strikes me in my immediate surroundings'. To what extent he had internalised Japanese graphic art can be inferred from the painting he made of an *Orchard in Blossom, Arles in the*

Background in April 1899: the trunks of the trees are rendered in lavender tints and outlined in black, just like those in the artist's painted copy after Hiroshige's plum.
The Van Gogh Museum preserves over 400 Japanese prints from the brothers' collection, many of them purchased from the noted dealer Siegfried Bing. Aside from the prints that inspired these pictures, Vincent's tracing of Hiroshige's plum also survives, which he made to facilitate the transition from print to painting.
The artist mounted both canvases in frames he himself painted with bright colours and decorated with calligraphic characters based on Japanese prints.

Vincent van Gogh
Japonaiserie: The Bridge in the Rain (after Hiroshige)
Canvas, 73 × 54 cm - summer/autumn 1887
Inv. S 114 V/1962 - F 372

On stylistic grounds the two canvases with skulls can be dated to the end of Vincent's Parisian period, but nothing is known about their original intention. They recall the drawings of skeletons he made in Antwerp, as well as the rather macabre picture of another smoking a cigarette. Though the skulls have been linked to the last self-portrait the artist painted in Paris, which contains references to death, it seems unlikely that the two works are more than studies, especially since they are devoid of props.

Vincent van Gogh
A Skull
Canvas, 43 × 31 cm - winter 1887/1888
Inv. S 123 V/1962 - F 297

Vincent van Gogh
A Skull
Canvas, 41.5 × 31.5 cm - winter 1887/1888
Inv. S 128 V/1962 - F 297a

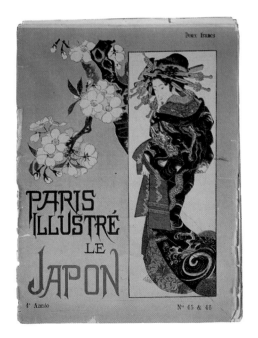

Cover of Paris Illustré: le Japon
May 1886

Van Gogh painted three Japonaiseries after Japanese prints. Though some have assumed they originally formed a single decoration, this seems unlikely given their divergent formats. The illustrated canvas is the largest of the three, and can be traced to a print by the Japanese artist Eisen. The print appeared on the cover of the May 1886 issue of the magazine *Paris Illustré* which was devoted to Japan. The same figure also occurs in the background of Van Gogh's portrait of the paint dealer Père Tanguy (Musée Rodin, Paris). Van Gogh himself fashioned an elaborate frame for the courtesan. It is decorated with cranes and frogs, both derogatory terms for prostitutes in French. The motif of the pond with water lilies and bamboo stalks seems to have been inspired by Hokusai, while the fat frog was modelled on a print by Utagawa Yoshimaru (1844-1907).

Vincent van Gogh
Self-portrait with Felt Hat
Canvas, 44 × 37.5 cm - winter 1887/1888
Inv. S 16 V/1962 - F 344

[I was] really broken, seriously ill and virtually an alcoholic'. The ambitious self-portrait of himself painting evokes his somber mood clearly. Dated 1888, the canvas is one of the last works Vincent painted before leaving for Arles. His description of the work in a letter to his sister Wil confirms the intense despondency he was feeling. 'A pinkish-grey countenance with green eyes, ashen hair, wrinkles in the forehead and around the mouth, stiff and wooden, a very red beard, rather untidy and sad, but the lips are full, a blue smock of rough linen and a palette with lemon-yellow, vermilion, Veronesque-green, cobalt-blue, in short, every colour except the orange beard on the palette, the only whole colours, however. The figure against a greyish-white wall.

'You'll say it looks a bit like the face of death in the book [*De kleine Johannes*, 1887] by [the Dutch author Frederik] van Eeden or something of the kind, good, but in the end, isn't such a figure – and it's not easy to paint oneself – in any case *something other* than a photograph? And you see, to my way of thinking Impressionism has this advantage over the rest, it's not trivial, and it seeks a deeper likeness than the photographer's'. The composition of the canvas has been compared to Cézanne's self-portrait at the easel. But in a letter to Emile Bernard of August 1888, Van Gogh himself referred to a self-portrait in the Louvre with a 'toothless laugh' by 'that old lion Rembrandt, a linen cloth on his head, palette in hand'.

The colour theory and stippled technique of the Neo-impressionists, with which Van Gogh became so well acquainted during his years in Paris, influenced his art in various ways. We have already seen how he employed the *pointille* in portraits and views of the capital, often to decorative ends. In this *Self-portrait with Felt Hat* of late 1887 or early 1888, he created a sort of aureole around himself using short lines or dashes. This personal variant of the Neo-impressionists' technique enabled him to determine the dynamic of a picture by simply varying the direction of his brushstrokes. In his eyes it was 'a real discovery'.

During his last months in Paris Van Gogh was deeply depressed. As he wrote Gauguin, 'When I left Paris

Vincent van Gogh
Self-portrait as Painter
Canvas, 65.5 × 50.5 cm - January 1888
Inv. S 22 V/1962 - F 522

Van Gogh in Arles

In February Van Gogh decided to leave Paris just as abruptly as he had come. He was drawn irresistably by the light of the south, and by the hope of finding something like Japan, the country that had captured his imagination in prints and novels. He also dreamed of organising an atelier for artists in the south – a dream that, with Gauguin's arrival in October 1888, seemed to have been realised. For reasons that have never become completely clear, he settled on the town of Arles. In one of his first letters to his brother from Provence he summarised what he had painted since making the move: 'an old Arlésienne, a landscape with snow, a view of a bit of pavement with a butcher's shop. The women here are very beautiful, that's absolutely true, unlike the museum in Arles, which is worthless [...]'.

This old woman was decidedly not one of the 'beautiful' Arlésiennes. The canvas recalls Emile Bernard's portrait of his grandmother, which Van Gogh had acquired from his friend in exchange for another work. As in that composition, a bed is summarily indicated in the background. *Old Woman from Arles*

harks back to the peasant types Vincent painted in Nuenen and then in Antwerp, under the influence of the 'tronies', or heads, of Frans Hals. But whereas Daumier and Gavarni had formed an important reference point when he painted his 'Heads of the People' in Nuenen, the expressive outlines of the old Arlésienne are patently inspired by Japanese prints, especially the actors' portraits in the brothers' collection.

Van Gogh's aspiration to become a figure painter and portraitist was finally realised in Arles. The important series of Zouave portraits, the postman Roulin, the peasant Patience Escalier and the 'Berceuse' all date from this period. Not until November 1888 did he paint a truly 'beautiful' Arlésienne, when he portrayed his friend Madame Ginoux in yellow and black.

Vincent van Gogh
Old Woman from Arles
Canvas, 58 × 42.5 cm -
February 1888
Inv. S 145 V/1962 -
F 390

Vincent van Gogh
Sprig of Almond Blossom in a Glass
Canvas, 24 × 19 cm - March 1888
Inv. S 184 V/1962 - F 392

Vincent van Gogh
Pear Tree in Blossom
Canvas, 73 × 46 cm - April 1888
Inv. S 39 V/1962 - F 405

These two small pictures, painted shortly after the artist's arrival in Arles, document the first signs of spring 1888. Van Gogh made another version of the almond sprig for his sister in early March. The charming canvas with a blossoming pear tree was conceived as the centrepiece of a tripartite decoration for the artist's brother.
It has much in common with a Japanese print, including the vertical format and the marked angularity of the young tree. The division of the background into clearly demarcated areas and the blue sky partitioned by trees likewise call Japanese woodcuts to mind. Yet when Theo wanted to exhibit the work at Boussod & Valadon's, Vincent objected; the canvas was 'all too innocent' for that.

Vincent van Gogh
The Langlois Bridge
Canvas, 59.5 × 74 cm - March 1888
Inv. S 27 V/1962 - F 400

The draw bridge shown here, called the Pont de Réginelle (or Réginal), was known locally as the 'Pont de Langlois', after the bridge-keeper. It is located south of Arles, where it spans a canal running from that city to Port-de-Bouc. At the far left can be seen the lock through which the canal empties into the Rhône. Van Gogh's objective was to amalgamate the Dutch character of the landscape, the light of the south, and the shapes sharply silhouetted against the sky which he associated with Japan.

He painted several versions of the composition in March 1888, in both oil and watercolour. The variant in the Van Gogh Museum is the last and simplest of all. The figures in the fore- and middle ground have been suppressed, and the bridge is seen at a greater distance, so as to stress the length of the canal and thus to accentuate the similarity of the landscape to that of the artist's native Holland. In May 1888 he would return to the theme of the drawbridge once again.

In the nineteenth century, painters frequently employed flowering fruit trees as symbols of spring. Van Gogh was certainly familiar with works by Daubigny and Millet in which such symbolism occurred. In a period of less than a month, between 24 March and 21 April 1888, Vincent produced a total of fourteen canvases describing blossoming fruit trees in Arles. He hoped these 'motifs everyone enjoys' would sell well and possibly also convince his countrymen that he was making progress. It was only after he had picked up his brush that the idea occurred to him of grouping the canvases into decorative triptychs. In a letter to his brother of about 13 April 1888 he summarised what he had in mind. 'I'd really like to make that set of nine canvases. You see, we can consider this year's nine canvases as an initial design for a much larger, definitive

Vincent van Gogh
Blossoming Peachtrees
Canvas, 80.5 × 59.5 cm - April 1888
Inv. S 25 V/1962 - F 404

Vincent van Gogh
Sketch of the orchard triptych
from a letter to Theo of ca. 13 April 1888

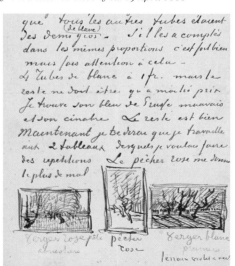

Vincent van Gogh
The Pink Orchard
Canvas, 64.5 × 80.5 cm - March/April 1888
Inv. S 26 V/1962 - F 555

decoration to be carried out at about the same time next year using exactly the same motifs'.

Apparently forgetting his hopes of selling the orchards for the time being, on 9 April he wrote his colleague Bernard that in painting the series he had followed 'no system of brushwork whatsoever':

'Thick layers of paint, bits of canvas with no paint, here and there completely un-finished areas, overpainted areas, rough areas – in short, I think the result is disturbing, and sufficiently shocking to scare off people with preconceived notions about technique'.

Judging from another letter to Bernard which he wrote on about 21 April 1888, Vincent's intention was to create an ensemble with a great variety of colour: 'I have a stack of nine orchards: a white one, a pink one, a pink one verging on red, a blueish-white one, a greyish-pink one and a green one with pink'. Yet he was constantly plagued by fears that the canvases did not measure up, that they were somehow unworthy of the term 'tableau'. He was quite taken with his *White Orchard*, however, and stipulated the sort of frame it should have: 'white, cold and hard'. Indeed in a letter to his brother of February 1889, he suggested submitting that very canvas to the Indépendants for their next exhibition. The Van Gogh Museum is proud to be the sole proprietor of three orchard paintings conceived by the artist as an ensemble and – unlike the others – never separated. The central canvas, *Blossoming Peachtrees*, is the second version of this motif. Vincent dedicated the first, which is now in the Rijksmuseum Kröller-Müller at Otterlo, to the memory of his recently deceased cousin Anton Mauve. After learning of Mauve's death, Vincent suggested that Theo send his widow a picture – 'something tender and very cheerful', he thought. The flowering trees were just what he had in mind.

How far Van Gogh had distanced himself from the grey palette of his former teacher in the meantime! As he wrote his sister in late March 1888, 'You will understand that it's not possible to paint the southern landscape using Mauve's palette, for instance. He belongs to the north and is, and will remain, a master of the grey. Nowadays the palette is very colourful, sky blue, orange, pink, vermilion, bright yellow, bright green, bright wine-red, violet. But by intensifying *all* the colours one comes back to peace and harmony. Something occurs in nature similar to what happens in Wagner's music, which, though played by a large orchestra, is nonetheless intimate'. Vincent would certainly have painted more orchards that spring, had it not been for the weather. 'The wind makes it very difficult for me to paint, but I secure my easel by driving stakes into the ground and then work regardless. It's too beautiful'.

To keep his brother abreast of his progress he sent coloured drawings of the pictures to Paris, taking care to point out that 'Of course the colours in the painted studies are brighter'. The illustrated watercolour with flowering peachtrees formed part of just such a shipment. Because certain pigments have faded somewhat in the meantime, the contrast between the paintings and the watercolour sketch is no longer as pronounced as it once was. In fact, because the canvases have faded the watercolour [see following page] probably gives a better idea of how colourful they were when they were freshly painted than do the canvases themselves.

Vincent van Gogh
The White Orchard
Canvas, 60 × 81 cm - April 1888
Inv. S 24 V/1962 - F 403

Vincent van Gogh
Blossoming Peachtrees
Black chalk and watercolour on paper,
45.5 × 30.5 cm - March 1888
Inv. D 208 V/1962 - F 1469

Vincent van Gogh
View of Arles with Irises in the Foreground
Canvas, 54 × 65 cm - May 1888
Inv. S 37 V/1962 - F 409

On 12 May 1888 Vincent wrote Theo about a landscape study he had just finished, a 'meadow full of bright yellow buttercups, a ditch with irises, green leaves and purple flowers, the town in the background, some grey willows, and a strip of blue sky. If the meadow doesn't get mowed, I'd like to do this study again, as the subject was very beautiful and I had some trouble getting the composition. A little town surrounded by fields all covered with yellow and purple flowers; exactly – can't you see it? – like a Japanese dream'. A week later he described the canvas to Bernard in virtually the same terms: 'That sea of yellow with a band of violet irises, and in the background that coquettish little town with its pretty women!'

Vincent van Gogh
The Sea at Les Saintes-Maries-de-la-Mer
Canvas, 51 × 64 cm - June 1888
Inv. S 117 V/1962 - F 415

One of the things that appealed to Van Gogh about living in Arles was the proximity of the Mediterranean. Yet it was not until late May that he actually visited the coast. At first he considered Marseilles, but finally settled on the picturesque fishing village of Les Saintes-Maries-de-la-Mer, where in the space of a few short days – from 30 May until 3 June – he produced no less than two seascapes, a village view and nine drawings.

Since his Scheveningen seascape of 1882, Vincent had painted no more 'marines'. Three sea and beach views constituted the fruits of his Mediterranean excursion. Two of these works are now in the Van Gogh Museum. Painted with speed and vigour, the illustrated seascape has all the marking of a picture painted *en plein air*. The bold red signature suggests the artist was satisfied with the results, and at the same time provides 'a red accent in the green'.

The canvas corresponds to Van Gogh's enthusiastic description of the sea: 'like the colour of mackerels, in other words changing – you don't always know if it's green or purple, you don't always know if it's blue, since before you know it the constantly shifting reflection has taken on a pink or a grey tint'.

Vincent van Gogh
Fishing Boats on the Beach at Les Saintes-
Maries-de-la-Mer
Canvas, 65 × 81.5 cm - June 1888
Inv. S 28 V/1962 - F 413

The view of the boats on the beach was done in the studio, based on a drawing made on the spot. As Vincent explained to Theo: 'When I went out very early in the morning, I made the drawing of the boats and am now making a painting of it, a size 30 canvas with more sea and sky on the right. That was before the boats departed in great haste, which I'd watched them do every morning but, since they leave so early, had no time to paint'.

Understandably the work, which is actually a bit smaller than Van Gogh told his brother, has been dubbed a 'still life with four boats'. The artist himself described the scene to Emile Bernard as 'small green, red and blue boats, so beautiful in form and colour that they remind one of flowers'. The stylised handling of the vessels betrays once more the influence of Japan. Van Gogh planned to make a second journey to Les Saintes-Maries but never returned. On 12 June he wrote his brother 'I haven't been back to Saintes-Maries; they've finished painting the house and I had to pay [...]'.

After the series of orchards and the never fully realised series of seascapes, Van Gogh focused his attention on peasant life during the summer of 1888. His first step in this direction was a series of wheatfields. The smaller of the two canvases shown here was probably painted within a matter of hours and has the character of an (albeit brilliant) sketch.

Around 12 June Vincent wrote Theo that he was working on a large, ambitious picture 'in the genre of the two landscapes of the Butte Montmartre', only 'stronger' and with 'slightly more style'. *The Harvest* shows the plain of La Crau outside Arles. In this panoramic landscape, painted from a lofty vantage point, it takes some effort to find the human activity that the title leads one to expect. At the left the composition is framed by the ruins of the fortified monastery of Montmajour and the Alpilles range.

As the orchards were an emblem of spring, so *The Harvest* symbolised summer. Van Gogh clearly found the Provençal landscape no less exciting once it 'began to get parched. There's old gold, bronze and copper in everything, and with the azure-green of the incandescent sky that gives a delicious, extraordinarily harmonious colour, with broken tints as with Delacroix'.

Van Gogh carefully prepared the work with detailed pen drawings. The canvas itself he painted 'in a single lengthy sitting', though he retouched it later.

Vincent van Gogh
Wheatfield
Canvas, 54 × 65 cm - June 1888
Inv. S 146 V/1962 - F 411

Vincent van Gogh
The Harvest
Canvas, 73 × 92 cm - June 1888
Inv. S 30 V/1962 - F 412

At an art gallery in Paris the Dutchman had seen a canvas with a similar harvest by Cézanne. Recalling that picture and comparing it to his own *Harvest*, he concluded that the French master had captured 'the hard side of Provence', and that there were therefore few essential parallels between the two works. 'I only want to say that Cézanne, like Zola, grew up in the countryside. He therefore knows it so well that in your head you have to make the same consideration to arrive at comparable tones. Obviously the two pictures could stand being juxtaposed, but they would have nothing in common'. Van Gogh felt more affinity with the landscapes of his fellow country-men, the seventeenth-century Dutch master Philips Koninck, who excelled at panoramas, than with Cézanne's.

For all Van Gogh's modesty, he was well aware that his depiction of the harvest on the plain of La Crau was in fact a masterpiece. To Theo he wrote not once but three times that 'The [...] canvas knocks absolutely all the others dead'.

Vincent van Gogh
The Zouave
Canvas, 65 × 54 cm - June 1888
Inv. S 67 V/1962 - F 423

From 20 until 23 June 1888 it did nothing but pour with rain in Arles. It was all the same to Vincent: 'I finally have a model – a Zouave – a bull-necked youth with a small face and the look of a tiger. I started out with one portrait and then did another. The half-length I painted of him was terribly garish – in a uniform the colour of blue enamelled saucepans, with faded reddish-orange passementerie and two lemon-yellow stars on the chest, an ordinary blue and very hard to do. I placed his feline, bronzed head with red hat against a green door and an orange brick wall. So it's a crude combination of colours that don't match, not easy to manage. The studies I made of it seem very harsh, but then I'd like to work on vulgar, even loud portraits like this all the time. I learn from it, which is what I most want from my work'.

In a similar vein Van Gogh described the work to his friend Emile Bernard, to whom he dedicated a watercolour drawing of the portrait: 'It is harsh and utterly ugly and badly done. Yet because I tackled genuine difficulties in it, it could clear the path for the future. The figures I make are almost always detestable in my own eyes and the more so in those of others; yet it's from studying the figure that you can learn the most'.

Vincent van Gogh
The Ploughed Field
Canvas, 72.5 × 92.5 cm - September 1888
Inv. S 40 V/1962 - F 574

During the summer of 1888 Van Gogh produced a great many landscapes. He considered the illustrated canvas one of the most successful, though the motif was 'nothing but clods of earth, the furrows in the colour of old wooden shoes under a forget-me-not blue sky with white flakes'. In his eyes this landscape was 'more peaceful' than the others. 'If the work always went so smoothly', he sighed in a letter to his brother, 'I would worry less about making money, for people would be drawn to it more readily if the technique were more harmonious'. Because of the heavily applied paint – 'the present studies are really made from a single *stream of paint*' – he realised the canvas would dry slowly. 'You have to treat pictures with thick impastos like strong wine: they have to rest'.

Vincent van Gogh
Vase with Sunflowers
Canvas, 95 × 73 cm - January 1889
Inv. S 31 V/1962 - F 458

In May 1888 Van Gogh rented 'the yellow house' on Place Lamartine, not far from the Rhône. He used the summer to put a fresh coat of paint on the building, where he already had his studio. It was there that the Zouave sat for him. For the interior the artist designed an ambitious decorative scheme in preparation for the arrival of Gauguin, the point being to make the house a 'refuge atelier' and a 'vrai maison d'artiste'. Knowing how much Gauguin liked the sunflower still lifes he had painted in Paris, in late August Vincent designed a decoration for his friend's room comprising no less than twelve of them, which he planned to frame in 'thin slats, painted in orange minium'. He threw himself into the project 'with the enthusiasm of someone from Marseilles eating bouillabaisse', but ultimately decided only two were worthy of his friend. But then they were – in Gauguin's words – 'a perfect example of a style that is completely Vincent'.

The *Vase with Sunflowers* in the Van Gogh Museum is actually a replica of one of the two pictures for Gauguin, painted by Van Gogh in January 1889. In February 1890 Vincent wrote the critic Albert Aurier that he saw the sunflowers as a symbol of 'gratitude'. In late September 1888 Van Gogh sent his brother a sketch of the picture he had just made of the Yellow House 'beneath a sulfur-yellow sun, beneath a sky of pure cobalt. [...] It's powerful, those yellow houses in the sun and then the incomparable brilliance of the blue. [...]

The pink house with green shutters on the left, standing in the shade of a tree, is the restaurant where I go to eat every day. My friend the postman lives at the end of the street on the left, between the two railroad bridges'.

Van Gogh called the canvas *The Street (La rue)*. Johannes Vermeer's *The Little Street* in Amsterdam's Rijksmuseum presumably suggested the title to him.

Vincent van Gogh
The Street (The Yellow House)
Canvas, 72 × 91.5 cm - September 1888
Inv. S 40 V/1962 - F 464

Vincent van Gogh
The Bedroom
Canvas, 72 × 90 cm - October 1888
Inv. S 47 V/1962 - F 482

On 16 October 1888 Van Gogh sent his brother a detailed description of the picture showing 'just my bedroom'. Having spent the entire summer painting feverishly outdoors, no wonder he was determined that the canvas evoke '*rest*', or '*sleep*'. The weary artist's sturdy furniture served to convey 'inviolable repose'. The austere interior of the yellow house reminded Vincent of the interiors painted by Johannes Bosboom, one of his favourite members of the Hague School, 'with the red tiles, the white walls, the pine or walnut furniture, the patches of vivid blue sky and the green seen through the windows'.

Shortly afterwards Van Gogh depicted a sturdy chair with rush seat like that at the left in *The Bedroom*. He placed it in the context of a symbolic self-portrait that took the form of a still life. He personified Gauguin in a similar fashion: as an armchair of a bit more elegant design. Whereas his own chair is rendered realistically by daylight, Gauguin's 'portrait' is a nocturne. The two modern novels and burning candle stand for his colleague's art, which relied more heavily on the imagination than his own.

Before going to Arles, Gauguin had spent some time working in Brittany. Paris was expensive for painters, and the constant exposure to new ideas could sometimes bewilder an impressionable artistic temperament. Hence the Frenchman's departure for the coast in early February 1888. The Bretons had long attracted painters of country life, who were intrigued by their picturesque traditions and costumes. Descended from Celts and living in isolation on their peninsula, the Bretons were considered pre-eminently 'primitive' and unspoilt, which explains their fascination for urban artists.

Intent on 'drinking in the character of the populace and the landscape', Gauguin moved into the pension Gloanec in Pont-Aven. In June 1888 he painted *La Ronde des petites Bretonnes*, showing girls dancing prettily while the hay was being made, a reprise of a theme he had previously treated in 1886. While a painted version of the composition shows the girls full length against a view of Pont-Aven, the illustrated pastel observes them at close range against a clear blue sky. The undulating outline follows the girls' movements as they dance.

In its present form the drawing was probably retouched after serving its original purpose as a study preparatory to the large painted versions of the same motif. Gauguin presented it to Theo van Gogh as a gift, out of gratitude for the 50 francs the dealer had sent him in Brittany.

The theme of dancing Breton girls subsequently became popular with members of the group of artists known as the Nabis, which included Maurice Denis, Paul Sérusier and Georges Lacombe.

Paul Gauguin
Paris 1848-1903 Atuana
Study of Breton Girls Dancing ('Ronde Breton')
Charcoal, pastel and watercolour, 24 × 41 cm -
1888
Inv. D 663 V/1963

Emile Bernard
Lille 1868-1941 Paris
Road in Brittany with Figures
Watercolour, 30.7 × 20.2 cm - July 1888
Inv. D 646 V/1962

Emile Bernard
Breton Woman in an Orchard
Watercolour, 32 × 19.1 cm - July 1888
Inv. D 645 V/1962

Though Emile Bernard had already been introduced to Gauguin in 1886 and the two artists had met again at the end of that summer in Brittany, it was only later that they began collaborating. It all started in July 1888, when Van Gogh wrote Bernard that Gauguin was in Pont-Aven. The two artists' subsequent meeting marked the beginning of a period of reciprocal influence. Around 23 July, Van Gogh thanked Bernard for sending him two colourful drawings of Breton women. 'I find the plane-tree road along the sea with two women talking in the foreground and figures walking very beautiful. Also the woman under the apple tree [...]'. Both sheets are executed in the Cloisonnist manner characteristic of the school of Pont-Aven. Their decorative – and occasionally also caricatural – conception anticipates the series of *Bretonnerie* prints Bernard would create in late 1888/early 1889. When, in late October 1888, Gauguin joined Van Gogh in Arles, he had with him a painting with Breton women by Bernard; Vincent was no less enthusiastic about that work, with its 'beautiful composition and – in all its naïveté – distinguished palette'.

Emile Bernard
Self-portrait with Portrait of Gauguin
Canvas, 46.5 × 55.5 cm - September 1888
Inv. S 206 V/1962

Van Gogh received these self-portraits – both painted in Pont-Aven in September 1888, where Bernard and Gauguin were living at the time – in Arles in early October. They were intended as expressions of friendship, albeit elicited by Vincent himself: having read that Japanese artists exchanged their work he had invited his friends to do the same. But rather than portraying one another as he had suggested – Bernard apparently shrank from the thought of painting his distinguished confrère, Gauguin – the two opted for self-portraits instead. Possibly as a concession to their Dutch colleague, they included each other's likenesses in the background. And in

Paul Gauguin
Self-portrait with Portrait of Bernard,
'Les Misérables'
Canvas, 45 × 55 cm - September 1888
Inv. S 224 V/1962

the lower left corner of his canvas
Bernard painted a Japanese print, an
allusion to the art form he had come to
know through his friend.
Van Gogh preferred Bernard's self-
portrait – 'a few simple tones, a few dark
lines, but [...] as elegant as a real, true
Manet' – to Gauguin's, which emanated
such melancholy as to alarm him. The

older artist had cast himself as Jean
Valjean, the protagonist of Victor Hugo's
novel *Les Misérables*, because like
Valjean, he fancied himself a social
outcast, and like Hugo's hero, he took
revenge 'by doing good'. By the same
token, his features evoke Valjean's
'nobility and inner gentleness. The
ruttish blood that floods the face and the

fiery hues enveloping the eyes are the
burning lava that makes our painter's
soul seethe'. Gauguin called the background 'feminine' on account of the
'child-like flowers', which stood for
artistic purity.

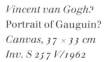

In the summer and autumn of 1888 Van
Gogh painted countless portraits,
especially members of the families
Ginoux and Roulin. After reaching Arles
on 25 October, Gauguin painted some of
the same models, including Joseph-
Michel Ginoux.
The identification of the figure seen at
an angle from behind with Gauguin has
been challenged, nor is the attribution
of the canvas to Van Gogh universally
accepted. On the other hand, it has been
argued that hardly any other artist
could be its author, the more so as we
can be certain the canvas once
belonged to Theo van Gogh.
The attitude of the figure is a credible
approximation of a painter at work, and

the German art historian Roland Dorn recognised the blurred outlines of Gauguin's *Woman in the Hay (Dans le foin)* in the background. In mid-November 1888 Vincent wrote his brother about that canvas, of which the Van Gogh Museum still preserves a watercolour study: 'Gauguin is working on a very original woman in the hay, with pigs. It promises to be very beautiful and to have great style'.

Van Gogh was painting sunflowers when Gauguin portrayed him in early December, placing one of his own landscapes in the background. The final result must have shocked Van Gogh, who supposedly exclaimed 'That's me, all right, but me as a madman'. In September 1889, Vincent confessed to his brother that he had been 'dead tired and extremely tense' when the portrait was painted.

Paul Gauguin
Paris 1848-1903 Atuana
Women on the Banks of the River, Tahiti
Canvas, 43.5 × 32.5 cm - 1892
Inv. S 222 V/1962

In December 1888 a 'huge catastrophe' occurred. There had been tension between Van Gogh and Gauguin while they were sharing the Yellow House in Arles. Exactly two months after the latter's arrival, on 23 December to be precise, the situation came to a dramatic head: Vincent threatened his friend with a knife. With characteristic self-control Gauguin just managed to escape. That same evening Vincent mutilated his ear and was promptly admitted to the local hospital; not until 7 January was he released. Gauguin left Arles immediately after the incident, putting an end to Van Gogh's dream of a 'southern atelier'.

After recovering from the crisis, at first Van Gogh was bitter about Gauguin's desertion. The two painters eventually made amends, however, and indeed Theo van Gogh remained Gauguin's dealer until his death in January 1891. In April 1891 Gauguin decided to leave Europe once again in search of an unspoilt society. This time he chose the South Pacific island of Tahiti, where in 1892 he painted this colourful landscape. About his initial hesitation to use strong colours Gauguin wrote in *Noa Noa*: 'the landscape, with its pure, intense colours astonished and blinded me [...]. Yet it was so simple to paint what I saw, to put a red or blue on my canvas without any premeditation! Golden shapes in the streams enchanted me: why did I hesitate, instead of letting all that gold and all that sunny joy flood my canvas?' In August 1893 Gauguin returned to Paris, bringing his first Tahitian adventure to an end.

Paul Gauguin
Paris in the Snow
Canvas, 71.5 × 88 cm - 1894
Inv. S 223 V/1962

Following the death of the Parisian art dealer Julien-François Tanguy in 1893, several Van Goghs owned by Gauguin found their way by mistake into the hands of Theo van Gogh's widow, who had been keeping some 200 of her brother-in-law's works with Tanguy. At Gauguin's request she promptly returned his property. Out of gratitude for her compliance the Frenchman sent her his *Paris in Winter*, along with his *Women by the River* of 1892.
Paris in the Snow is a surprisingly 'Impressionist' picture. It was painted in February 1894 in homage to the late painter Gustave Caillebotte, who had helped the fledgling artistic movement get on its feet. After lengthy public discussion his important collection had finally been accepted by the French State. In 1878 Caillebotte himself had painted a *View of Rooftops, Effect of Snow* (Musée d'Orsay, Paris), to which Gauguin's depiction of the view from his studio on Rue Vercingétorix seems to refer. Considering it is a snowscape, his canvas is remarkably colourful.

In June 1888 Van Gogh sought to realise a dream he had long cherished: he painted his own version of Millet's *Sower*, which had fascinated him ever since he first picked up a brush. Yet the artist was not satisfied with the results, an ambitious amalgamation of things observed and imagined. He went on changing many of the details of the picture (now in the Rijksmuseum Kröller-Müller) till finally he concluded it was a 'flop': the large format notwithstanding, the Otterlo canvas was nothing more than a 'glorified study' in his eyes. In the course of 1888 he continued to produce several variants,

until in late November he made his last attempt to improve on his hero's masterpiece: 'another sower. Large lemon-yellow disc as sun. Yellow-green sky with pink clouds. The earth violet, the sower and the tree Prussian blue; size 30 canvas'. The smaller version of the composition in the Van Gogh Museum illustrated here is probably a study for the work, which is now in the Bührle Collection, Zurich. In reply to a favourable letter from his brother Vincent indicated that he, too, was satisfied with the results: 'Occasionally a canvas becomes a painting, like *The Sower*, which I, too,

think is better than the first'. The placement of the figure's head against the sun lends the work a certain religious air. The prominent arrangement of the tree is usually traced to Gauguin's *Vision after the Sermon: Jacob Wrestling with the Angel* (Edinburgh, National Gallery), which features a similar diagonal, but the composition could just as easily have been inspired by a Japanese print.

'I've made portraits of *an entire family*', Vincent wrote Theo with evident satisfaction in early December 1888, 'the family of the postman [Roulin], whose head I've done before: husband, wife, baby, the small boy and the 16-year-old son, all types and really French, though they look like Russians. Size 15 canvases. [...] I hope to go on with this and to paint more serious poses and pay for them with portraits. And if I manage to make *that entire family* better still, then at least I'll have done something to my own liking'. Though the illustrated portraits are smaller than those the artist mentioned in his letter, which were painted in late November, not much time could have elapsed between the execution of the two groups.

Since Camille Roulin, 'the small boy' Vincent referred to in his letter, was born in July 1877, he would have been eleven when this portrait was painted. Another version of it hangs in the Philadelphia Museum of Art. Little Marcelle was born on 31 July 1888; three versions of her likeness are known.

Vincent sent the baby's portrait to Theo in Paris in May 1889. On 5 July Theo's wife Jo, who was expecting a child, wrote her brother-in-law that everyone admired the canvas. Indeed the couple was so pleased with the portrait that they hung it in such a way that 'from my place at table I have a perfect view of the child's big blue eyes, lovely little hands and round cheeks. I like to think that our baby will be just as strong, just as healthy and just as beautiful – and that one day his uncle will want to make a portrait of him!' Marcelle must indeed have had a healthy constitution, for she died only in 1980, at the age of 91!

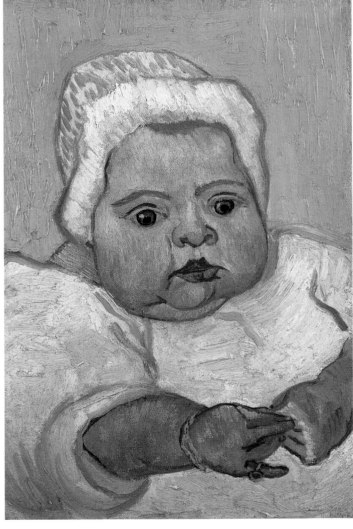

Vincent van Gogh
Orchard in Bloom
Canvas, 72.5 × 92 cm - April 1889?
Inv. S 38 V/1962 - F 511

In the spring of 1889 Van Gogh resolved to take up his series of blossoming orchards once again, only to be delayed by his admission to the hospital following a subsequent breakdown. On 24 March 1889 he wrote his brother that he expected to be back at work before long, and by early April he was ready to begin. Around the tenth of the month he sent his friend Paul Signac a sketch of the orchard with the silhouette of Arles in the background. The picture itself – 'almost entirely green, with a bit of lilac and grey' – had been painted on a rainy day.

In mid-April Vincent wrote Theo that he had already finished six studies, 'including two large orchards. I'm in a great hurry, because those effects are so ephemeral'. By the time he wrote his sister at the end of the month, however, the artist was clearly disappointed: 'Last year I made ten or twelve orchards and this year I have only four, so the work isn't going very well'. When exactly the large illustrated orchard was painted is uncertain. Some have argued it was made the previous year, but the style has more in common with the orchards Vincent painted in the spring of 1889.

Vincent van Gogh
Orchard in Bloom with Arles in the Background
Canvas, 50.5 × 65 cm - April 1889
Inv. S 36 V/1962 - F 515

This closely observed bit of nature belongs to a series of studies of flowers and clumps of grass. Though difficult to date, the canvases were probably painted toward the end of Vincent's stay in Arles. In August 1888 he had made several studies of dusty thistles along the side of a road, all of the same format. The illustrated picture may be one of the 'spring studies' he wrote Theo about in April 1889.

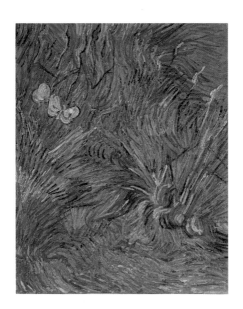

Vincent van Gogh
Garden with Flowers and Two White Butterflies
Canvas, 55 × 45.5 cm - spring 1889
Inv. S 110 V/1962 - F 402

Vincent van Gogh
Steps in the Garden of St Paul's Hospital in St-Rémy
Black chalk, pencil, ink and watercolour,
62 × 44.5 cm - May 1889
Inv. D 438 V/1962 - F 1535

Van Gogh in St-Rémy

On 8 May Van Gogh arrived by train at the mental hospital St-Paul-de-Mausole in St Rémy-de-Provence, which he and Theo had chosen. Dr Peyron, to whose care the artist had entrusted himself, inscribed the following diagnosis in his book of patients: 'Though at this moment he appears to have fully regained his senses, he feels he lacks the strength and courage to live independently, and has therefore asked to be admitted to this institution of his own accord. In light of his previous history I have come to the conclusion that Mr van Gogh suffers from epileptic fits, and that it would be advisable to keep him under observation here for a good while'. At the end of the first fortnight, Dr Peyron informed Theo that Vincent was doing well: 'He spends the whole day drawing in the garden'. The doctor had promised the artist that he could work outside the walls of the asylum as soon as his condition stabilised. Peyron confided to Theo, however, that his brother's chances of a lasting recovery were slim, 'since I have good reason to believe the attack he had is caused by a form of epilepsy. If this proves to be the case, we must fear the worst'. In mid-July Van Gogh's illness struck again, while he was painting in a field. It was not until late August that he regained his strength. At that point, while confined to his room, he started painting a series of copies after prints by Millet as well as a number of portraits. In late September he ventured forth from the institution again, this time to paint the surrounding hills and olive orchards and the main street of St-Rémy. But more attacks followed in December and January. Despite the constant assaults on his mental health, Vincent sent no less than seven shipments of pictures to Theo from St-Rémy. The 'bright yellow note' of Arles gave way to a more subdued palette, which the artist himself associated with a yearning for the north. Qualitatively the sojourn in St-Rémy signified anything but a decline. It was there that Van Gogh produced a magnificent series of olive orchards and cypresses, as well as views of the surrounding hills – such as *The Reaper* – and flower still lifes like *The Irises*.

Vincent van Gogh
Trees and Bushes in the Garden of St Paul's
Hospital at St-Rémy
Watercolour and gouache, 46.5 × 62 cm - May 1889
Inv. D 334 V/1962 - F 1533

Vincent van Gogh
Olive Grove
Canvas, 45.5 × 59.5 cm - June 1889
Inv. S 44 V/1962 - F 709

In the peaceful surroundings of St Paul's Hospital in St-Rémy, Van Gogh's fear of insanity gradually subsided. The confrontation with his fellow patients reconciled him with the fate of other artists who had had to struggle with their psyches, such as Matthijs Maris, Monticelli and Méryon. 'I see those artists regain their calm aura and can you imagine how much it means to rediscover old confrères?'
In the immediate proximity of the asylum there were several small olive groves. Starting in June, Vincent made some attractive studies of them, though as he wrote his brother he found the motif 'very difficult'. His goal was to capture the characteristic qualities of the olive trees in the hope that this quintessentially Provençal motif would become 'a personal impression [...] just as the sunflowers are for the yellow tints'. In a letter to Bernard he compared the silvery grey of the olive trees with that of Corot, but even the French master had not captured their essence: 'it has never been done before, whereas various artists have managed to paint apple trees and willows, for instance'. Vincent also drew inspiration from his fellow patients. The so-called 'one-eyed' man, assigned by some scholars to his Arles period, whom the artist portrayed in 1889, was certainly one of the inmates. No sooner did he receive it in May 1890 as part of a shipment of pictures from St-Rémy than Theo liked the canvas, which he dubbed the 'fellow with the puffy face'.

Vincent van Gogh
The Man with the Puffy Face
Canvas, 56 × 36 cm - 1889
Inv. S 113 V/1962 - F 532

Vincent van Gogh
Ivy
Canvas, 73 × 92.5 cm - July 1889
Inv. S 51 V/1962 - F 746

Since Van Gogh was not permitted to leave the hospital garden when he was first in St-Rémy, he had to content himself with whatever motifs he could find within its walls. Fortunately there were plenty of picturesque nooks from which to choose. The tall pines towered over the 'tall and untidy grass [...] mixed with all sorts of periwinkel', on which the sun shining through the trees created fascinating patterns of light and shade. In a letter to his brother of 6 July Vincent mentioned this size 30 canvas for the first time. It later became a favourite of Jo van Gogh, who loved 'the delicious coolness and freshness of the *sousbois*. I feel like I know that spot and have been there often – I love it so much'. Indeed her affection for the picture was so great that the family held on to it.

In mid-July 1889 Van Gogh was felled by another serious attack in St-Rémy. Not until 22 August was he able to write again, at which point he informed his brother that the illness had overcome him near the entrance to a quarry 'while I was painting in the field on a windy day'. Despite the attack he managed to finish the canvas. The colours were gloomy: 'dull and subdued, broken green, red and rust-coloured yellow ochres'. Though he had painted it in summer, he associated the work with the north. He painted another quarry in October 1889, but opted for the more colourful palette native to Japanese art in that case.

On 22 May 1889 Vincent wrote Theo that he had just drawn 'a large, rather rare moth, called a death's-head moth, with amazingly fine colours: black, grey, subtle white with a red reflection (or a hint of olive green). It is very large. To paint it I first had to kill it, which was a pity as it was such a beautiful animal'. Besides the drawing Vincent described, the Van Gogh Museum also preserves a sketch Vincent made of the same insect for Theo. In the definitive painting he portrayed it on an arum flower. There is also a superb reed pen study of a similar flower in the Museum.

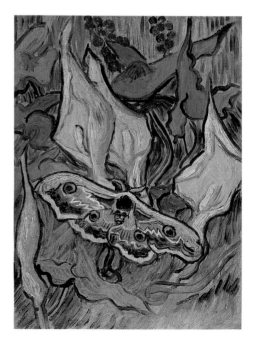

Vincent van Gogh
Wheatfield with Reaper
Canvas, 73 × 92 cm - September 1889
Inv. S 49 V/1962 - F 618

On 2 July 1889 Vincent announced that he was working on a 'wheatfield with a small reaper and a large sun. The canvas is completely yellow, save for the wall and the background with purple hills'. After another attack interrupted him later that month he finally finished in September. Dissatisfied with the outcome, he plunged into the second version, shown here, which he finished around 4 September. Thinking his mother would be able to grasp the picture – 'as simple as one of those crude woodcuts you find in farmer's almanacs' – he made a smaller replica for her and his sister Wil (now in the Folkwang Museum, Essen). 'In this reaper – a vague figure working like the devil in the intense heat to finish his task – I then saw the image of death, in the sense that the wheat being reaped represents mankind. So if you will it's the opposite of the sower I've attempted in the past. But there's nothing sad about this death: it happens in broad daylight, under a sun that bathes everything in a fine, golden light'.

Vincent van Gogh
Reaper with Sickle
Canvas, 43.5 × 33.5 cm
Inv. S 198 V/1962 - F 687

_____

The Sheaf-binder
Canvas, 44.5 × 32 cm
Inv. S 173 V/1962 - F 693

The Sheaf-binder
Canvas, 43 × 33 cm
Inv. S 172 V/1962 - F 700

_____

Peasant Woman Beating Flax
Canvas, 40.5 × 26.5 cm
Inv. S 43 V/1962 - F 697

The Thresher
Canvas, 44 × 27 cm
Inv. S 171 V/1962 - F 692

The Sheep Shearers
Canvas, 43 × 29 cm
Inv. S 42 V/1962 - F 634

The Woodcutter
Canvas, 43.5 × 25 cm
Inv. S 170 V/1962 - F 670

A print by Adrien Lavieille after Millet
with ten scenes of country life formed
the inspiration for Vincent's series of as
many small paintings, seven of which
are still in the Van Gogh Museum. In a
moment of crisis in September 1889 he
sought to regain his bearings by copying
the work of the French master. Most of
the prints he copied meticulously,
alternating the vertical formats at times
with slightly more horizontal ones, and
devising his own background for the
sheaf-binder. Blue and yellow
predominate, the two colours Vincent
most associated with peasant life.

Vincent van Gogh
Window of Van Gogh's Studio in St Paul's
Hospital at St-Rémy
Black chalk and gouache, 62 × 47.6 cm - 1889
Inv. D 337 V/1962 - F 1528

Vincent van Gogh
The Vestibule of St Paul's Hospital at St-Rémy
Black chalk and gouache, 61.5 × 47.4 cm - 1889
Inv. D 176 V/1962 - F 1530

ST-RÉMY

Vincent van Gogh
The Falling of the Leaves
Canvas, 73.5 × 60.5 cm - October 1889
Inv. S 46 V/1962 - F 651

Both of these paintings describe autumnal views of the garden of St Paul's Hospital at St-Rémy. The canvas with the lonely figure walking among tangled, Art Nouveau-like trees Vincent called *The Falling of the Leaves*. The work evinces painstaking observation, but also exemplifies Vincent's 'search for style [...] more virile and more powerful'.

Van Gogh described the large, sketch-like canvas with the garden of the asylum, which is actually the second version of the composition, in a letter to Emile Bernard: 'on the right a grey terrace, a bit of the house. Several overblown rosebushes, on the left the garden – red ochre – parched by the sun, covered with pine needles. The

edge of the garden is planted with large pines with red-ochre trunks and branches, as well as green foliage darkened with a mixture of black. The tall trees stand out against the evening sky in yellow intersected by purple stripes; the yellow becomes pink and green at the top. A wall – likewise red-ochre – obstructs the view and only

a purple and yellow-ochre hill rises above it. The first tree has an enormous trunk, but was struck by lightning and cut down. One branch, however, still sticks up very far and a rain of dark green needles is falling. That austere giant – his pride wounded – stands, if you give him the character of a human being, in contrast to the false smile of a last rose on the nearly overblown bush opposite it'.

A self-portrait of the tormented artist can be read into this description, yet the picture is also an implicit critique of themes recently painted by Gauguin and Bernard, which were far removed from visual reality. Van Gogh wanted to prove to them 'that you can express a feeling of anxiety without immediately referring to the historical Gethsemane'.

This copy after Millet is modelled on an etching by Alfred Delaunay. The composition can be traced to a picture Millet painted in three versions between 1862 and 1864, called *Winter: the Plain of Chailly*. The lack of figures distinguishes the work *vis-à-vis* the rest of Millet's oeuvre. The plough and harrow lying in the field are the only references to human activity, which came to a standstill in winter. Possibly because Delaunay's etching was unclear, the setting of Van Gogh's painting is more wintry than that of Millet's, and the effect even more desolate as a result. He blanketed the earth with a layer of snow and called the canvas *Le champ sous la neige*. In May 1890 Theo congratulated Vincent on the Millet copies, 'perhaps the most beautiful you've made'.

'I have the feeling that painting after those drawings by Millet is more a question of *translating them into another language* than of copying them', Vincent wrote his brother in November 1889. Theo concurred when he received the canvas in early January: 'Copied like this it is no longer a copy. There's a tone to it and everything is so beautifully surrounded with sky'.

The Evening Hour formed part of a set of four large pictures after Millet's *Heures de la journée*. Van Gogh painted the peasant interior – modelled again on a print by Lavieille – 'in a gamut of soft purples and lilacs'. He used bright colours to suggest radiant light within the dark interior, in contrast to the dark tonality of his Nuenen period, as exemplified by *The Potato Eaters*.

Possibly encouraged by the success of *The Evening Hour*, in late April 1890 Vincent considered 'redoing the picture of the peasants at table, by lamplight. By now that canvas must be altogether black; perhaps I can do it over completely from memory'.

Vincent van Gogh
A Small Stream in the Ravine, 'Les Peiroulets'
Canvas, 32 × 41 cm - October 1889
Inv. S 118 V/1962 - F 645

Vincent van Gogh
Bird's-eye View of an Olive Grove
Canvas, 33.5 × 40 cm - November/December 1889
Inv. S 148 V/1962 - F 716

The three oil studies illustrated here are among Van Gogh's lesser known works. Though somewhat exceptional within his oeuvre, they do have two things in common: all of them presumably date from the fourth quarter of 1889, and evince the author's abiding love for Japanese art, which survived his internment in St-Rémy.

Both chromatically and thematically, the brightly coloured brook in the ravine 'Les Peiroulets' is related to the large canvas *The Path through the Ravine* (of which there are versions in the Boston Museum of Fine Arts and the Rijksmuseum Kröller-Müller, Otterlo). Vincent associated the vivid colours of these works with Japan. He enjoyed the 'autumnal effects with their rich colouring, the green skies contrasting with yellow, orange and green trees and bushes, the bits of earth in every shade of purple [...]'.

In a letter to his friend Emile Bernard, Van Gogh remarked that his draughtsmanship and the large planes of colour which distinguished his work at the time occasionally recalled the

Vincent van Gogh
Field with Two Rabbits
Canvas, 32.5 × 40.5 cm - autumn/winter 1889
Inv. S 99 V/1962 - F 739

artists of Pont-Aven. This certainly applies to the bird's-eye view of olive trees winding through a landscape. Here, the Japanese character is sooner determined by the decorative treatment of the subject than by the colour scheme. Playful rabbits in their natural surroun-

dings are a motif that recurs frequently in Japonism. They figure, for instance, in prints by Henri Guérard, who illustrated Louis Gonse's *L'Art Japonais*, and in those of Lucien Pissarro, whose wood engraving with rabbits belonged to the Van Gogh brothers' collection.

Vincent van Gogh
Olive Grove
Canvas, 73 × 92 cm - November 1889
Inv. S 45 V/1962 - F 707

While searching for 'somewhat contrasting effects of foliage, which constantly changes colour with the tints of the sky', Van Gogh produced no less than ten canvases with olive groves during his stay in St-Rémy. 'The effect of daylight, of sky is such that countless motifs can be gotten out of the olive trees', he wrote in May 1890. Irritated by the abstractions of his former comrades Gauguin and Bernard, in late 1889 he sought inspiration for his studies of olive groves in the work of Corot and Impressionists such as Monet and Renoir. In art he believed olive groves were destined to become an important theme: 'probably it won't be long before olive trees will be painted in every conceivable fashion, as the willow and the Dutch pollard willow have been, and the Norman apple tree ever since Daubigny and Cézar de Cock painted it'.

Vincent van Gogh
Pietà (after Delacroix)
Canvas, 73 × 60.5 cm - September 1889
Inv. S 168 V/1962 - F 630

Vincent van Gogh
The Raising of Lazarus (after Rembrandt)
Canvas, 50 × 65 cm · May 1890
Inv. S 169 V/1962 · F 677

In St-Rémy, Vincent copied not only after Millet, but after Daumier, Delacroix, Doré and Rembrandt as well. From Delacroix's oeuvre he chose the *Good Samaritan* and the *Pietà*. In describing his copy after the latter to his sister Wil, he wrote that the Mater Dolorosa had the 'good respectable hands of a working woman', and not an unfeeling, classical countenance, but 'the pale exterior, the vague, perplexed look of someone utterly exhausted by anxiety, weeping and sleeplessness'. In token of his recovery from a relapse in late February 1890, which had incapacitated him for two months, in May 1890 Vincent painted a canvas with

an apposite biblical theme. The work is a free interpretation of a detail from Rembrandt's etching *The Raising of Lazarus*, which focuses on the reviving Lazarus and his two sisters. 'The cave and the corpse are violet, yellow and white. The woman removing the cloth from the face of the figure who's just been revived wears a green dress and has orange hair, while the other has black hair and wears a green-and-pink-striped dress. Behind them a landscape with blue hills and a yellow ascendant sun. As such the combination of colours has the same significance as the chiaroscuro of the etching'. Just as the Lazarus – like the Christ in the *Pietà* – is

a thinly veiled self-portrait, both of the female figures unmistakeably represent Van Gogh's solicitous friends from Arles, Mesdames Ginoux and Roulin. Were they available as models, he wrote his brother, 'then I would certainly try and paint this canvas on a larger scale, since they resemble the [biblical] characters I imagined them to be'. Remarkably enough, the figure of Christ in Rembrandt's composition is replaced by the sun in Van Gogh's.

Vincent van Gogh
Enclosed Field with the Alpilles in the Background
Canvas, 37.5 × 30.5 cm - February 1890
Inv. S 417 M/1990 - F 723

Like many of the other small canvases in his oeuvre, this Alpilles landscape, which entered the Museum in 1990 as part of the Ribbius-Peletier Bequest, is not mentioned in Van Gogh's correspondence. It is usually dated to June 1889, the period in which he painted several large-scale versions of the same landscape. Yet the fact that the trees at the foot of the mountains are in bloom suggests that it was actually made months later, in the early spring of 1890. After all, when Van Gogh arrived in St-Rémy on 8 May 1889, the trees were no longer flowering. The canvas therefore must have been created at about the same time as the *Almond Branches in Blossom*, probably as a colour study for a more ambitious work which was never realised.

Vincent described the motif to his brother shortly after being admitted to the asylum on 22 May 1889: 'Through the window with iron bars I can see an enclosed wheatfield, a prospect similar to a picture by Van Goyen'. In early June he was already working on a large canvas showing the view 'from the window of my bedroom. In the foreground a ruined cornfield that was beaten to the ground by a thunderstorm. A wall as enclosure and on the other side the grey leaves of a few olive trees, cottages and hills. [...] It is an extremely simple landscape – also as regards colour'.

Just after the baby's birth on 31 January 1890, Theo informed his brother that he was now the father of a healthy son named Vincent Willem. On 9 February he added that the child had blue eyes 'like the baby you painted with round cheeks'. Vincent promptly painted a picture for the proud parents' bedroom, showing 'Large branches of almond blossoms against a blue sky'. He apparently drew inspiration from Japanese prints, which so often contain the same motif. While the artist was briefly in Paris on 18 May 1890, en route to Auvers, he enjoyed seeing his white almond blossoms hanging above the piano in his brother's apartment.

As in Arles, Van Gogh decided to resume his series of blossoming trees in St-Rémy in the spring of 1890, only to have his plans frustrated once again by

illness. Having scarcely recovered from one attack, he was struck by another as he was finishing the illustrated canvas, which left him with no choice but to lay down his brush for two months. He could not have been more surprised by this latest setback, since he had just painted the almond blossoms 'with calm and meticulous brushwork'. Now he saw his hopes for the series dashed. 'I fell ill while working on the almond blossoms', he wrote his brother in April. 'Had I been able to continue, you can well imagine I would have done more trees in blossom'. 'Now the trees have all but stopped blossoming; really, I have no luck'.

Vincent van Gogh
Cottages and Cypresses Beneath a Stormy Sky
Canvas on panel, 29 × 36.5 cm - March/April 1890
Inv. S 112 V/1962 - F 675

Though Van Gogh usually stopped working whenever he was ill, he made countless drawings after Brabant motifs during the attack of March-April 1890, thus expressing his nostalgia for the north. As he wrote his mother and sister in late April, 'while my illness was at its worst, I carried on painting regardless, including a souvenir of Brabant, cottages with moss roofs and copses of beech, on an autumn evening with stormy sky, the red sun setting in reddish clouds'. He made these 'souvenirs of the north' from memory, but asked his brother and mother to send him old studies and drawings for inspiration. 'Though they are not good in and of themselves, they can help me remember things and serve as material for new work'. He kept his word while staying in Auvers, where he painted new versions of such Nuenen themes as *The Cottage* and *The Church Tower*. The cypresses are especially striking in this 'Souvenir du Nord'. Aside from olive trees, Van Gogh considered them the pre-eminent symbol of Provence: 'with respect to line and proportion, every bit as beautiful as an Egyptian obelisk. And the green is so extraordinary. It is the *black* note in a sunny landscape, but it is one of the most interesting black notes, so far as I can imagine one of the most difficult to get down on canvas well. You should see them here against the blue, or rather *in* the blue'.

The critic Albert Aurier made some flattering remarks about Vincent's cypresses – 'their silhouettes pointing upward like nightmares of black flame' – in an article that appeared in January 1890. In gratitude, the artist presented him with one of his most ambitious treatments of the motif, which is now in the Rijksmuseum Kröller-Müller. He had already started working on the canvas in the summer of 1889, but been interrupted by an attack in July. The smaller of the two pictures illustrated here is a replica of it.

In early June Van Gogh wrote from Auvers that he had been 'working very hard lately in St-Rémy, on floral bouquets in particular: roses and purple irises'. Altogether he painted four large flower pieces, possibly hoping to match the success he had achieved with a similar picture of irises at the Salon des Indépendants. *Vase with Irises* is an excellent example of 'enormously divergent complementary colours, which stand out all the more strongly because of their contrasts'. The three small nature studies, which once more betray strong Japanese influence, date from the same spring.

Vincent van Gogh
Butterflies and Poppies
Canvas, 34.5 × 25.5 cm -
Inv. S 188 V/1962 - F 748

Vincent van Gogh
Wild Roses
Canvas, 24.5 × 33 cm -
Inv. S 190 V/1962 - F 597

Vincent van Gogh
Roses and a Beetle
Canvas, 33.5 × 24.5 cm
Inv. S 187 V/1962 - F 749

Vincent van Gogh
Vase with Irises against a Yellow Background
Canvas, 92 × 73.5 cm - May 1890
Inv. S 50 V/1962 - F 678

Vincent van Gogh
Ears of Wheat
Canvas, 64.5 × 48.5 cm - June 1890
Inv. S 88 V/1962 - F 767

Van Gogh in Auvers

The last seventy days of his life Vincent van Gogh spent just north of Paris in the small town of Auvers-sur-Oise. More than once the artist had expressed his longing for the north while still living in St-Rémy. After lengthy correspondence on the subject with Theo he finally settled on Auvers, where the physician Paul Gachet would keep an eye on him. Alongside his medical practice Gachet also did a bit of painting. He and Monticelli had been friends, and his collection testified to his contact with such artists as Cézanne, Guillaumin, Pissarro and Renoir.

It was Dr Gachet who also introduced Vincent to the art of etching; the ensuing experiments resulted in an etched portrait of Gachet. Though they only lay some thirty kilometres from Paris and were popular with Parisians, Auvers and nearby Pontoise were known primarily as rural art colonies. Besides the aforementioned Cézanne and Pissarro, Daubigny had lived and worked there as well. The extraordinarily large number of paintings, drawings and sketchbook scribblings Van Gogh produced during this period attest to his inquisitiveness about his new surroundings, which were 'of a grave beauty'.

The long crisis he had endured between February and April 1890 in St-Rémy certainly made him no less susceptibile to new impressions, depicting both the picturesque village and the wheatfields in the outstretched landscape of the Ile-de-France. He used the 'close-up' of cornstalks as a background for a study of a peasant girl, inspired by his lifelong models Millet and Breton. In a letter to Gauguin of mid-June 1890 he described the painting: 'nothing but ears of corn, greenish-blue stalks, long, ribbon-like leaves, green and pink on account of the reflection [...]. They are greens of varying quality, of the same colour value, so that they form a green entity which owing to the vibration recalls the soft noises of the ears of corn swaying back and forth in the wind'.

Vincent van Gogh
Portrait of Dr Paul
Gachet
'L'homme à la pipe'
Etching 18 × 15 cm -
June 1890
Inv. P 469 V/1962 -
F 1664

Travelling from Paris Vincent reached Auvers on 20 May. Three days later he wrote his brother that he was 'doing very well these days. I'm working hard, and have done four painted studies and two drawings. You'll see a drawing of an old vineyard with the figure of a peasant woman which I'm thinking of turning into a large canvas'. The two drawings have been kept together and are now in the Van Gogh Museum. Though his plans for a painted version of the *Old Vineyard with Peasant Woman* apparently came to naught, he did produce several canvases showing the picturesque houses of Auvers. The two illustrated drawings have been called 'symphonies in purple-blue'. It is not

Vincent van Gogh
Landscape with Cottages
Pencil and watercolour, 45 × 54.5 cm - May 1890
Inv. D 332 V/1962 - F 1640 r

clear, however, what inspired Van Gogh's use of the shade, since there is no longer any trace of it in his painted versions of such motifs. Both drawings were executed vigorously *en plein air* and later retouched in the studio. The drawings perpetuate the theme of thatched-roof cottages from Vincent's 'Souvenirs du Nord'. No sooner had he arrived in Auvers than he noticed them: 'Auvers is very beautiful – among other things [there are] many thatched roofs, something that's becoming rare. By doing a few canvases of them very conscientiously I hope to have some chance of covering my living expenses [...] it's truly rural, characteristic and picturesque'.

Vincent van Gogh
Old Vineyard with Peasant Woman
Pencil and watercolour, 43.5 × 54 cm - May 1890
Inv. D 446 V/1962 - F 1624

Vincent van Gogh
View of Auvers
Canvas, 50 × 52 cm - May/June 1890
Inv. S 105 V/1962 - F 799

Auvers was very popular with painters. On Corot's advice, Daubigny had settled there in the late 1850s; in the '70s, the Impressionists Guillaumin and Pissarro spent time there as well. In the collection of his friend Dr Gachet, Van Gogh could see for himself how Cézanne had previously portrayed the town and artists were still working in Auvers by the time Vincent arrived. While it is true he narrowly missed the French painter Louis Dumoulin, who was known for his 'Japanese work', he was able to spend several days with Walpole Brooke; having grown up in Japan, the Australian artist must have fascinated the Dutchman.

So much did Vincent enjoy the tranquil village that he tried to convince Theo to leave Paris, thinking it would do him good – be it for only a month – to bring his family and enjoy the 'peacefulness à la Puvis de Chavannes'. As if to entice his brother he noted the 'numerous villas and modern bourgeois houses, very gay in the sun with lots of flowers'.

Shortly after arriving in Auvers, Vincent wrote his brother 'Word has it that Mme Daubigny and Mme Daumier still live here – at least I know for certain the former does'. Daubigny, one of Van Gogh's favourite painters, had built a house in Auvers in 1861, where indeed his widow still resided. As early as 17 June the Dutch artist had 'an idea for a larger canvas of Daubigny's house and garden, of which I've already done a small study'. That study has much in common with the Impressionists' handling of such garden scenes. Yet it was not till late July that Theo was shown a sketch of the completed work, in the last letter he was to receive from his brother.

Vincent made two versions of *Daubigny's Garden*, which he himself considered one of his 'most intensely felt works'. Both are painted on horizontal canvases measuring 50 x 100 cm, a format he alone employed in Auvers. For this particular study, showing only the right half of the definitive composition, he chose a square canvas exactly half that size.

Vincent van Gogh
The Garden of Daubigny (study)
Canvas, 50.7 × 50.7 cm - June 1890
Inv. S 104 V/1962 - F 765

The series of large bouquets of roses and irises he painted just before leaving St-Rémy was Van Gogh's last major project in this genre. Most of the still lifes he produced in Auvers are modest studies, which for all their simplicity make a nonetheless daring impression. Their composition is usually very informal and surprisingly modern. The illustrated still life is one of the most peaceful in the series; it reiterates the composition of the large still lifes *Sunflowers* and *Irises* on a smaller scale. The manner seems to have been influenced by a flower piece Cézanne painted in 1873 which belonged to Dr Gachet. The work now hangs in the Musée d'Orsay, Paris.

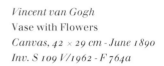

Vincent van Gogh
House with Two Figures
Canvas, 38 × 45 cm - May/June 1890
Inv. S 108 V/1962 - F 806

Vincent van Gogh
Vase with Flowers
Canvas, 42 × 29 cm - June 1890
Inv. S 109 V/1962 - F 764a

Vincent van Gogh
Two Pear Trees with the Château of Auvers
Canvas, 50 × 101 cm - June 1890
Inv. S 107 V/1962 - F 770

When it came to architecture, Van Gogh rarely tried his hand at anything grandiose. His taste ran to humble cottages on the whole, and when he chose religious architecture as a motif, he generally preferred village churches over cathedrals. In Arles, for instance, he ignored virtually all the architecture of note, including the imposing Roman ruins. It was exactly the same story in Auvers: aside from the local church and the small town hall, he confined himself to modest vernacular architecture. At first glance the illustrated canvas with the seventeenth-century château of Auvers appears to be an exception to the rule, but on closer inspection it becomes clear that the summer evening, not the château, is the subject. Vincent described the picture, which he finished shortly before 24 June, as 'an evening effect: two pear trees completely black against a yellowing sky, with cornfields and in the purple background the château surrounded by dark foliage'. The composition resembles an elongated version of one of the last blossoming orchards he painted in Arles, just as the charged, melancholic atmosphere and the silhouette-like forms recall some of his desolate Drenthe and Nuenen landscapes. Van Gogh may have been thinking of Charles Daubigny, who specialised in evocative landscapes at dusk. Indeed he could have seen many of the French master's works in the collection of the Hague painter-collector Willem Mesdag, which comprised more Daubignys than any other outside France.

Vincent van Gogh
Wheatfields Beneath Thunderclouds
Canvas, 50 × 100.5 cm - July 1890
Inv. S 106 V/1962 - F 778

———————————

Vincent van Gogh
Crows in the Wheatfields
Canvas, 50.5 × 103 cm - July 1890
Inv. S 149 V/1962 - F 779

When Vincent briefly visited Paris on 6 July 1890, Theo informed him he was contemplating leaving Boussod & Valadon and going into business for himself. Vincent already had qualms about burdening his brother, and now that Theo's plans threatened his precarious finances, the situation became unbearable. Theo's wife Jo sought to reassure her disconsolate brother-in-law, to which he responded around 10 July:
'My dear brother and sister, Jo's letter was really like a gospel to me, a deliverance from the agony caused by the hours I'd shared with you, which were a bit too difficult and trying for us all. It was quite something when we all felt our daily bread was in danger, quite something when we realised that for other reasons as well our existence is so vulnerable. Back here, I was still very

sad and continued to feel the storm that threatens you weighing on me, too. What can we do? I generally try to be fairly cheerful, you know, but the very foundation of my life is also threatened, and now my situation is likewise insecure'. Though he himself claimed the brush nearly fell from his hand, back in Auvers Van Gogh painted two 'enormous outstretched wheatfields beneath angry skies, and I have consciously tried to express sadness and extreme loneliness in them'. These landscapes with heavily overcast skies have inspired the most disparate interpretations. Especially because the *Wheatfield with Crows* was long mistaken for Van Gogh's last work, it has been seen as a premonition of his suicide on 29 July 1890. Yet the true tenor of these works is altogether different, and – notwithstanding the

gloom – positive: 'I'm all but certain that in those canvases I have formulated what I cannot express in words, namely how healthy and heartening I find the countryside'. The landscapes belong to a series of twelve canvases of the same horizontal format, collectively forming a paen to country life. As such, the cycle fulfilled an ambition the artist had cherished even before leaving Holland. The Art Nouveau-like canvas with the tortured tree roots is an astonishingly modern, almost abstract work. Yet it is not the first of its kind in Vincent's oeuvre. It was preceded by the drawing *Les Racines*, executed during his Hague period in 1882, which was an attempt to visualise 'the struggle of life'.

Vincent van Gogh
Tree Roots
Canvas, 50 × 100 cm - July 1890
Inv. S 195 V/1962 - F 816

Joseph Mendes da Costa
Amsterdam 1863 - 1939 Amsterdam
Vincent van Gogh
Bronze, 13.5 × 39 cm
Inv. V 49 V/1981

Epilogue

Following her brother-in-law's death in July 1890 and then her husband's in January 1891, Jo van Gogh was left in Paris with the brothers' collection as well as the sizeable legacy of Vincent's paintings and drawings. She eventually decided to take her infant son Vincent Willem and the whole collection with her to the Netherlands. At that point she threw herself into promoting the art of her late brother-in-law, lending his work to numerous exhibitions, those at the Haagsche Kunstkring in 1892 and Amsterdam's Stedelijk Museum in 1905 being only the most important. Through the German dealer Paul Cassirer, Vincent's work was also shown repeatedly in Germany, where it attracted a great many collectors. In 1914, moreover, Jo's edition of Vincent's letters to Theo appeared and was subsequently translated into other languages. After her death in 1925, her son continued where Jo left off.
The mythology surrounding Van Gogh would have it that his genius was utterly misunderstood at the time of his death. The tragedy, rather, was that his death coincided with his breakthrough. The fact is that Vincent's work was favourably

received at exhibitions in Paris and Brussels while he was still alive, as evidenced by the enthusiastic review written by Albert Aurier. After his death, the artists Emile Bernard in France and Jan Toorop in the Netherlands joined Jo van Gogh in fostering the fame of the late artist. Thanks in part to their efforts, his oeuvre was regularly exhibited in the 1890s and inspired many young artists. Around the turn of the century, when Impressionism experienced a second florescence, the so-called 'Fauves' in France and the German Expressionists let themselves be influenced by the work of Van Gogh. Along with Gauguin, Seurat and Cézanne, the Dutch master was now proclaimed one of the 'fathers of modern art'.

Johan Cohen Gosschalk
Zwolle 1873-1912 Amsterdam
Portrait of Jo van Gogh-Bonger
Pencil and coloured chalk, 37 × 27 cm - 1902
Inv. D 791 T/1982

Bibliography

General nineteenth century

Robert Rosenblum et al., *Art of the Nineteenth Century. Painting and Sculpture*, New York 1984

Gabriel Weisberg, *The Realist Tradition: French Painting and Drawing 1830-1900*, Cleveland 1980

Ronald de Leeuw et al., *The Hague School: Dutch masters of the 19th century*, London 1983

Carel Blotkamp et al., *The age of Van Gogh: Dutch painting 1880 - 1895*, Zwolle 1990

Sophie Monneret, *L'Impressionnisme et son époque*, Paris 1978

John Rewald, *Post-Impressionism from Van Gogh to Gauguin*, New York 1956

John House et al., *Post-Impressionism. Cross-Currents in European Painting*, London 1979

Patricia Eckert Boyer et al., *The Nabis and the Parisian Avant-Garde*, New Brunswick 1988

Geneviève Lacambre et al., *French Symbolist Painters. Moreau, Puvis de Chavannes, Redon and their followers*, London 1972

Van Gogh: general

J.-B. de la Faille, *The works of Vincent van Gogh. His paintings and drawings*, Amsterdam 1970

Jan Hulsker, *The complete Van Gogh: paintings, drawings, sketches*, New York 1980

Jan Hulsker, *Vincent and Theo van Gogh: a dual biography*, Ann Arbor 1985

Louis van Tilborgh et al., *Vincent van Gogh: paintings*, Milan 1990

Griselda Pollock, *Vincent van Gogh in zijn Hollandse jaren. Kijk op stad en land door Van Gogh en zijn tijdgenoten 1870-1890*, Amsterdam 1980

Evert van Uitert et al., *Van Gogh in Brabant. Paintings and drawings from Etten and Nuenen*, Zwolle 1987

Bogomila Welsh-Ovcharov, *Vincent van Gogh. His Paris period 1886-1888*, Utrecht 1976

Bogomila Welsh-Ovcharov et al., *Van Gogh à Paris*, Paris 1988

Bogomila Welsh-Ovcharov, *Vincent van Gogh and the birth of Cloisonism*, Toronto 1981

Ronald Pickvance, *Van Gogh in Arles*, New York 1984

Ronald Pickvance, *Van Gogh in St. Rémy and Auvers*, New York 1986

Tsukasa Kodera, *Vincent van Gogh, Christianity versus Nature*, Amsterdam & Philadelphia 1990

Louis van Tilborgh et al., *Van Gogh & Millet*, Zwolle 1988

Tsukasa Kodera et al., *Vincent van Gogh and Japan*, Kyoto & Tokyo 1992

Roland Dorn et al., *Vincent van Gogh and the modern movement 1890-1914*, Freren 1990

John Rewald, 'Theo van Gogh as art dealer' in: *Studies in Post-Impressionism*, 1986, pp. 7-115

Van Gogh: letters

Han van Crimpen et al., *De brieven van Vincent van Gogh*, The Hague 1990

Douglas Cooper, *Paul Gauguin: 45 Lettres à Vincent, Théo et Jo van Gogh. Collection Rijksmuseum Vincent van Gogh, Amsterdam*, The Hague & Lausanne 1983

Cahiers Vincent

Published in collaboration with the Vincent van Gogh Foundation

1. Fieke Pabst, *Vincent van Gogh's poetry albums*, Zwolle 1988

2. Walter Feilchenfeldt, *Vincent van Gogh & Paul Cassirer, Berlin. The reception of Van Gogh in Germany from 1901 to 1914*, Zwolle 1988

3. Cornelia Peres et al., *A Closer Look: Technical and Art-Historical Studies on Works by van Gogh and Gauguin*, Zwolle 1991

4. Ronald Pickvance, *'A great artist is dead'. Letters of Condolence on Vincent van Gogh's Death*, Zwolle 1992

5. Louis van Tilborgh et al., *The Potato Eaters by Vincent van Gogh*, Zwolle 1993

The collection of the Van Gogh Museum

Evert van Uitert et al. (eds.), *The Rijksmuseum Vincent van Gogh*, Amsterdam 1987

Johannes van der Wolk, *The seven sketchbooks of Vincent van Gogh: a facsimile edition*, New York 1986

Josefine Leistra, *George Henry Boughton: God Speed! Pelgrims op weg naar Canterbury*, Zwolle 1987

Ronald de Leeuw, *The Van Gogh Museum, Paintings and Pastels*, Zwolle 1994

Charlotte van Rappard-Boon et al., *Catalogue of the Van Gogh Museum's collection of Japanese prints*, Zwolle 1991

Ronald de Leeuw et al., *Van Gogh Museum. Aanwinsten/Acquisitions 1986-1991*, Zwolle 1991

Catalogues of exhibitions held in the Van Gogh Museum: a selection

Ronald Pickvance et al., *Monet in Holland*, Zwolle 1986

Ellen Wardwell Lee et al., *Neo-impressionisten: Seurat tot Struycken*, Zwolle 1988

Gianna Piantoni et al., *Ottocento/Novecento: Italiaanse kunst 1870-1910*, Zwolle 1988

Patricia Eckert Boyer et al., *L'Estampe originale: artistic printmaking in France, 1893-1895*, Zwolle 1991

MaryAnne Stevens et al., *Emile Bernard 1868-1941: a pioneer of modern art*, Zwolle 1990

Aimée Brown-Price, *Puvis de Chavannes*, Zwolle 1994

Ronald Pickvance, *Degas sculptor*, Zwolle 1991

Series 19th-century Masters

1. Ronald de Leeuw, *Philippe Rousseau 1816-1887*, Amsterdam & Zwolle 1993

2. Lucas Bonekamp, *Louis Welden Hawkins 1849-1910*, Amsterdam & Zwolle 1993

3. Charlotte van Rappard-Boon, *Félix Bracquemond 1833-1914*, Amsterdam & Zwolle 1993

4. Ian Millman, *Georges de Feure 1869-1943*, Amsterdam & Zwolle 1993

Hernri de Toulouse-Lautrec
Albi 1864-1901 Malromé
Portrait of Vincent van Gogh
Pastel on cardboard, 57 × 46.5 cm - 1887
Inv. D 693 V/1962

Van Gogh chronology

1853   Vincent van Gogh is born in Zundert on 30 March, the eldest son of the preacher Theodorus van Gogh (1822-1885) and Anna Cornelia Carbentus (1819-1907).

1857   His brother Theo is born on 1 May.

1869   Van Gogh joins the international art dealers Goupil & Cie in The Hague.

1872   His correspondence with Theo begins.

1873   In June Vincent is transferred to the firm's London branch, where he works until 15 May 1875.

1875   He is transferred – against his will – to Paris.

1876   Vincent is dismissed by Boussod & Valadon, who succeeded Goupil & Cie. He becomes a teacher at a boarding school in Ramsgate in mid-April. In July he moves to Isleworth, where as an assistant preacher he delivers his first sermon in October.

1877   Through April 1877 he works in a bookshop in Dordrecht. In May he moves to Amsterdam and prepares to study theology.

1878   In May Vincent abandons his studies in Amsterdam. He later moves to the Belgian Borinage to do evangelical work.

1880   Van Gogh decides to become an artist.

1881   In April Vincent moves in with his parents in Etten, where he spends much of his time drawing figures. His love for his cousin Kee Vos is unrequited.
In late November he moves to The Hague to study under his cousin Anton Mauve.

1882   In The Hague he rents a studio on Schenkweg. His relationship with Sien Hoornik, unmarried and pregnant, contributes to his falling out with Mauve. His uncle, the art dealer C.M. van Gogh, commissions twelve drawings with views of The Hague from him.

1883   His relationship with Sien Hoornik having come to an end, on 11 September Vincent leaves for the province of Drenthe. He concentrates on landscape. In early December he opts to go to his parents, who have moved to Nuenen in the meantime.

1884   Following in the footsteps of J.F. Millet, Van Gogh decides to become a painter of peasant life, and in January begins work on a series of weavers.

1885   He paints a series of fifty peasant heads, which ultimately lead to *The Potato Eaters*, his first 'masterpiece'.
His father, the Rev. Theodorus van Gogh, dies on 26 March. On 24 November the artist leaves for Antwerp, where he is influenced by the work of Rubens.

1886   Works after the model at the Antwerp academy, but finds the training pedantic. About 1 March Van Gogh leaves unexpectedly for Paris, where he moves in with his brother Theo, now the manager of the Montmartre branch of Goupil's. For three months he works in the studio of Fernand Cormon.
Van Gogh paints views of Montmartre and experiments with colour in the form of flower still lifes. He becomes acquainted with the work of Monticelli and the Impressionists.

1887   Vincent buys Japanese prints from Siegfried Bing and art supplies from Père Tanguy. His intimates include Louis Anquetin, Emile Bernard, Lucien Pissarro and Paul

Signac. In March/April he organises an exhibition of Japanese prints at the Café du Tambourin.

In the summer he works on the banks of the Seine and in the new suburb of Asnières.

1888 The busy life of Paris exhausts Van Gogh and on 19 February, in search of sun and relaxation, he sets out for the south. Quite by chance he lands in Arles (Provence).

In April Vincent paints a series of blossoming orchards.

In May he rents the 'Yellow House' but does not move in till autumn.

He visits the Mediterranean fishing village of Saintes-Maries-de-la-Mer. That summer he paints scenes of life on the land, *Harvest in La Crau* being the highpoint.

In anticipation of the arrival of his friend and colleague Paul Gauguin, who plans to share the 'southern atelier' with him, in August Van Gogh paints the *Sunflowers* to decorate the Yellow House.

Not until 23 October does Gauguin arrive. The two artists work side by side on landscapes for a time, but their personalities and artistic outlook are so different that they inevitably fall out. Van Gogh threatens Gauguin with a knife and on 23 December cuts off a piece of his own ear. He is admitted to the hospital in Arles.

1889 Having recovered, on 7 January Van Gogh returns to the Yellow House.

In February the inhabitants of Arles turn against Van Gogh. He is subsequently re-admitted to the hospital.

On 17 April Theo marries Johanna ('Jo') Bonger, the sister of his friend Andries.

In May Van Gogh places himself under the care of Dr Peyron at the asylum St-Paul-de-Mausole in nearby St-Rémy. His olive orchards and cypresses date from this period. While painting *Entrance to a Quarry*, however, he suffers yet another attack.

That autumn Van Gogh paints his *Reaper*, which incorporates the wheat field he could see from his room. He regains his self-confidence painting copies after works by Delacroix, Millet and Rembrandt.

1890 In December and January Van Gogh must endure further attacks, each of which lasts for one week. Meanwhile his reputation grows steadily.

On 31 January Theo's son is born and named after his uncle Vincent Willem. The Belgian artist Anna Boch buys one of Vincent's pictures from Theo.

In late February Van Gogh undergoes another crisis, this one lasting until late April. He now returns to motifs from his Nuenen period, entitled 'souvenirs of the north'.

In mid-May Van Gogh leaves for the village of Auvers-sur-Oise near Paris. On his way through the capital he finally meets his sister-in-law Jo.

In Auvers, the physician and amateur painter Paul Gachet keeps an eye on Vincent. The artist takes a room at the inn of Ravoux and proceeds to paint the small houses of the village with their thatched roofs, the town hall and the church.

His principal landscapes, now painted on a new, double-square format, describe the outstretched wheat fields around Auvers.

On 27 July Van Gogh shoots himself in the chest and dies two days later in the company of Theo. Among the mourners at his funeral on 30 July are Bernard, Lucien Pissarro and Tanguy.

1891 Theo dies on 25 January. Jo van Gogh returns to the Netherlands with the brothers' art collection.

1892 The first Van Gogh exhibition in the Netherlands at the Haagsche Kunstkring.

1905 A large Van Gogh exhibition is mounted in the Stedelijk Museum, Amsterdam, where much of the collection of Dr Vincent Willem van Gogh is displayed from 1930.

1914 Jo van Gogh publishes Vincent's collected letters to Theo.

1962 Establishment of the Vincent van Gogh Foundation.

1973 Opening of the Van Gogh Museum in Amsterdam.

Colophon

Publisher:
Waanders Uitgevers, Zwolle

Design:
Gijs Sierman, Amsterdam

Translation:
Andrew McCormick

Printer:
Waanders Drukkers, Zwolle

Photos:
Vincent van Gogh-Foundation, Amsterdam with the exception of:
Rijksdienst Beeldende Kunst, The Hague (p. 13)
Stedelijk Museum, Amsterdam (p. 8)
Van Gogh Museum, Amsterdam (pp. 6, 8-13, 19-21, 29, 54, 144)

With many thanks to the Vincent van Gogh Foundation

CIP-gegevens Koninklijke Bibliotheek, Den Haag

Leeuw, Ronald de

Van Gogh at the Van Gogh Museum / Ronald de Leeuw. – Zwolle :
Waanders. – Ill.
Met lit. opg.
ISBN 90-6630-492-8
NUGI 921/911
Trefw.: Gogh, Vincent van / schilderkunst ; Nederland ;
geschiedenis ; 19e eeuw.